3rd Edition

파고다교육그룹 언어교육연구소 | 저

PAGODA TOEFL

Actual Test Writing

PAGODA Books

3rd Edition

PAGODA TOEFL Actual Test Writing

초　　판 1쇄 발행 2014년 12월 15일
개정 2판 1쇄 발행 2021년 2월 26일
개정 3판 1쇄 인쇄 2025년 4월 21일
개정 3판 1쇄 발행 2025년 4월 30일

지 은 이 | 파고다교육그룹 언어교육연구소
펴 낸 이 | 박경실
펴 낸 곳 | **PAGODA Books** 파고다북스
출판등록 | 2005년 5월 27일 제 300-2005-90호
주　　소 | 06614 서울특별시 서초구 강남대로 419, 19층(서초동, 파고다타워)
전　　화 | (02) 6940-4070
팩　　스 | (02) 536-0660
홈페이지 | www.pagodabook.com

ISBN 978-89-6281-940-3 (13740)

파고다북스 www.pagodabook.com
파고다 어학원 www.pagoda21.com
파고다 인강 www.pagodastar.com
테스트 클리닉 www.testclinic.com

낙장 및 파본은 구매처에서 교환해 드립니다.

2023년 7월
New iBT TOEFL®의 시작!

TOEFL 주관사인 미국 ETS(Educational Testing Service)는 iBT TOEFL® 시험에서 채점되지 않는 더미 문제가 삭제되면서 시간이 개정 전 3시간에서 개정 후 2시간 이하로 단축됐으며, 새로운 라이팅 유형이 추가되었다고 발표했다. 새로 바뀐 iBT TOEFL® 시험은 2023년 7월 26일 정기 시험부터 시행된다.

- 총 시험 시간 기존 약 3시간 ⋯› 약 2시간으로 단축
- 시험 점수는 각 영역당 30점씩 총 120점 만점으로 기존과 변함없음

영역	2023년 7월 26일 이전	2023년 7월 26일 이후
Reading	지문 3~4개 각 지문 당 10문제 시험 시간 54~72분	지문 2개 각 지문 당 10개 시험 시간 36분
Listening	대화 2~3개, 각 5문제 강의 3~5개, 각 6문제 시험 시간 41~57분	28문제 대화 2개, 각 5문제 강의 3개, 각 6문제 시험 시간 36분
Speaking	*변함없음 4문제 독립형 과제 1개 통합형 과제 3개 시험 시간 17분	
Writing	2문제 통합형 과제 1개 독립형 과제 1개 시험 시간 50분	2문제 통합형 과제 1개 수업 토론형 과제 1개 시험 시간 30분

목차

이 책의 구성과 특징

>> New TOEFL 변경사항 및 최신 출제 유형 완벽 반영!

2023년 7월부터 변경된 새로운 토플 시험을 반영, iBT TOEFL®의 출제 경향을 완벽하게 반영한 문제와 주제를 골고루 다루고 있습니다.

>> 예제를 통한 문제 유형별 공략법 정리!

본격적으로 실전에 들어가기에 앞서, iBT TOEFL® Writing의 2가지 문제 유형과 예시 답변을 정리해 자주 나오는 질문을 파악하고 iBT TOEFL® 전문 연구원이 제시하는 고득점 답변 필수 전략을 학습할 수 있도록 구성했습니다.

>> TOEFL Writing에서 자주 사용하는 핵심 표현 정리!

각 문제 유형별로 답변에서 자주 사용하는 핵심 표현들을 예문과 함께 정리해, 시험장에 가기 전 핵심 표현만 다시 한 번 손쉽게 확인할 수 있도록 준비했습니다.

>> 7회분의 Actual Test로 실전 완벽 대비!

실제 시험과 동일하게 구성된 7회분의 Actual Test를 수록해 실전에 철저하게 대비할 수 있도록 구성했습니다.

>> 추가 3회분의 Actual TEST 온라인으로 제공!

교재 외에 추가 3회분의 Actual TEST를 파고다북스 홈페이지에서 PDF로 다운로드 받으실 수 있습니다. (총 10회분의 Actual TEST 제공)

>> 그룹 스터디와 독학에 유용한 단어 시험지 생성기 제공!

자동 단어 시험지 생성기를 통해 교재를 학습하면서 외운 단어 실력을 테스트해 볼 수 있습니다.

▶ 사용 방법: 파고다북스 홈페이지(www.pagodabook.com)에 로그인한 후 상단 메뉴의 [모의테스트] 클릭 > 모의테스트 메뉴에서 [단어 시험] 클릭 > TOEFL - PAGODA TOEFL Actual Test Writing을 고른 후 원하는 문제 수를 입력하고 문제 유형 선택 > '단어 시험지 생성'을 누르고 별도의 브라우저 창으로 뜬 단어 시험지를 PDF로 내려 받거나 인쇄

>> 무료 MP3 다운로드 제공

파고다북스 홈페이지(www.pagodabook.com)에서 교재 MP3 다운로드 가능합니다.

▶ 이용 방법: 파고다북스 홈페이지(www. pagodabook.com)에서 해당 도서 검색 > 도서 상세 페이지의 '도서 자료실' 코너에 등록된 MP3 자료 다운로드(로그인 필요)

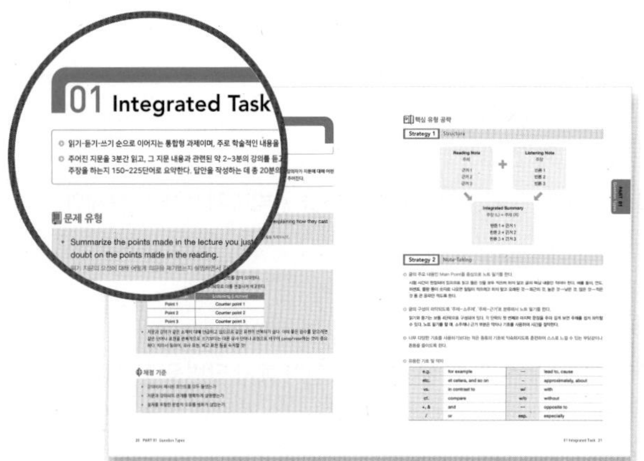

PART 01. Question Types

iBT TOEFL® 전문 연구원이 제안하는 문제 유형별 고득점 전략을 학습하고, 각 문제 유형별로 답변에서 자주 사용하는 핵심 표현들을 예문과 함께 익힐 수 있습니다.

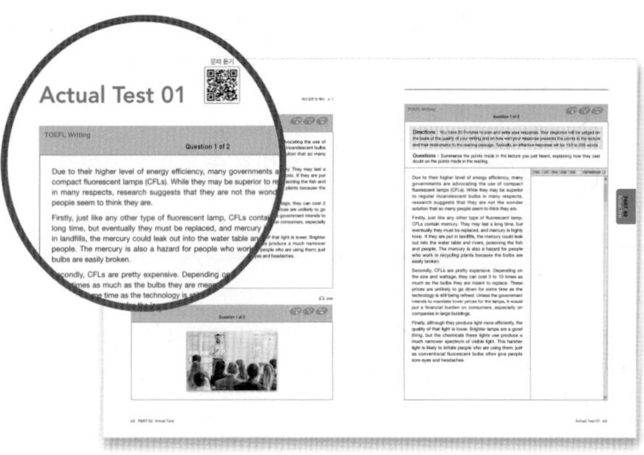

PART 02. Actual Tests

실제 시험과 동일하게 구성된 7회분의 Actual Test를 통해 실전에 대비합니다.

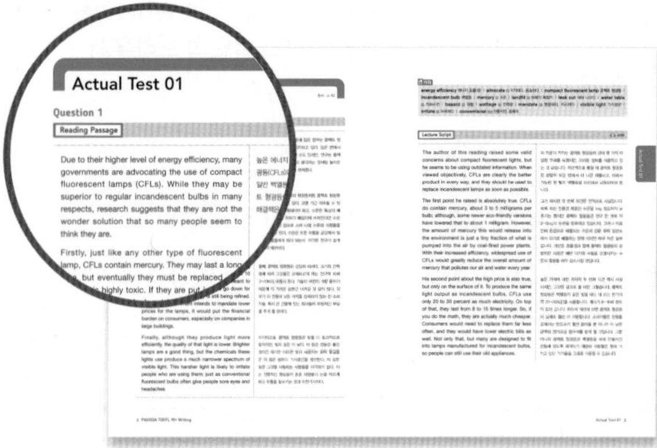

예시 답변 및 해석

읽기/듣기 지문 및 해석, 질문에 대한 예시 답변, 주요 어휘 정리를 수록했습니다.

4주 완성 학습 플랜

DAY 1	DAY 2	DAY 3	DAY 4	DAY 5
PART 01				
01 Integrated Task • 문제 유형 및 전략 • Sample Question	01 Integrated Task • Sample Question 다시 보기 • 자주 사용하는 핵심 표현 암기	01 Academic Discussion Task • 문제 유형 및 전략 • Sample Question 1 • Sample Question 2	01 Academic Discussion Task • Sample Question 3 • Sample Question 4 • Sample Question 5	01 Academic Discussion Task • Sample Questions 다시 보기 • 자주 사용하는 핵심 표현 암기
DAY 6	**DAY 7**	**DAY 8**	**DAY 9**	**DAY 10**
PART 02				
Actual Test 01 • 문제 풀이	Actual Test 01 Review • 문제 & 답변 다시 보기 • 표현 및 단어 암기	Actual Test 02 • 문제 풀이	Actual Test 02 Review • 문제 & 답변 다시 보기 • 표현 및 단어 암기	Actual Test 03 • 문제 풀이
DAY 11	**DAY 12**	**DAY 13**	**DAY 14**	**DAY 15**
PART 02				
Actual Test 03 Review • 문제 & 답변 다시 보기 • 표현 및 단어 암기	Actual Test 04 • 문제 풀이	Actual Test 04 Review • 문제 & 답변 다시 보기 • 표현 및 단어 암기	Actual Test 05 • 문제 풀이	Actual Test 05 Review • 문제 & 답변 다시 보기 • 표현 및 단어 암기
DAY 16	**DAY 17**	**DAY 18**	**DAY 19**	**DAY 20**
PART 02				
Actual Test 06 • 문제 풀이	Actual Test 06 Review • 문제 & 답변 다시 보기 • 표현 및 단어 암기	Actual Test 07 • 문제 풀이	Actual Test 07 Review • 문제 & 답변 다시 보기 • 표현 및 단어 암기	PART 02 Review • 문제 & 답변 다시 보기 • 학습한 표현 및 단어 총정리

iBT TOEFL® 개요

1. iBT TOEFL® 이란?

TOEFL은 영어 사용 국가로 유학을 가고자 하는 외국인들의 영어 능력을 평가하기 위해 개발된 시험이다. TOEFL 시험 출제 기관인 ETS는 이러한 TOEFL 본연의 목적에 맞게 문제의 변별력을 더욱 높이고자 PBT(Paper-Based Test), CBT(Computer-Based Test)에 이어 차세대 시험인 인터넷 기반의 iBT(Internet-Based Test)를 2005년 9월부터 시행하고 있다. ETS에서 연간 30~40회 정도로 지정한 날짜에 등록함으로써 치르게 되는 이 시험은 Reading, Listening, Speaking, Writing 총 4개 영역으로 구성되며 총 시험 시간은 약 2시간이다. 각 영역별 점수는 30점으로 총점 120점을 만점으로 하며 성적은 시험 시행 약 4~8일 후에 온라인에서 확인할 수 있다.

2. iBT TOEFL®의 특징

1) 영어 사용 국가로 유학 시 필요한 언어 능력을 평가한다.

각 시험 영역은 실제 학업이나 캠퍼스 생활에 반드시 필요한 언어 능력을 측정한다. 평가되는 언어 능력에는 자신의 의견 및 선호도 전달하기, 강의 요약하기, 에세이 작성하기, 학술적인 주제의 글을 읽고 내용 이해하기 등이 포함되며, 각 영역에 걸쳐 고르게 평가된다.

2) Reading, Listening, Speaking, Writing 전 영역의 통합적인 영어 능력(Integrated Skill)을 평가한다.

시험이 4개 영역으로 분류되어 있기는 하지만 Speaking과 Writing 영역에서는 [Listening + Speaking], [Reading + Listening + Speaking], [Reading + Listening + Writing]과 같은 형태로 학습자가 둘 또는 세 개의 언어 영역을 통합해서 사용할 수 있는지를 평가한다.

3) Reading 지문 및 Listening 스크립트가 길다.

Reading 지문은 700단어 내외로 A4용지 약 1.5장 분량이며, Listening은 3~4분 가량의 대화와 6~8분 가량의 강의로 구성된다.

4) 전 영역에서 노트 필기(Note-taking)를 할 수 있다.

긴 지문을 읽거나 강의를 들으면서 핵심 사항을 간략하게 적어두었다가 문제를 풀 때 참고할 수 있다. 노트 필기한 종이는 시험 후 수거 및 폐기된다.

5) 선형적(Linear) 방식으로 평가된다.

응시자가 시험을 보는 과정에서 실력에 따라 문제의 난이도가 조정되어 출제되는 CAT(Computer Adaptive Test) 방식이 아니라, 정해진 문제가 모든 응시자에게 동일하게 제시되는 선형적인 방식으로 평가된다.

6) 시험 응시일이 제한된다.

시험은 주로 토요일과 일요일에만 시행되며, 시험에 재응시할 경우, 시험 응시일 3일 후부터 재응시 가능하다.

7) Performance Feedback이 주어진다.

온라인 및 우편으로 발송된 성적표에는 수치화된 점수뿐 아니라 각 영역별로 수험자의 과제 수행 정도를 나타내는 표도 제공된다.

3. iBT TOEFL®의 구성

시험 영역	Reading, Listening, Speaking, Writing
시험 시간	약 2시간
시험 횟수	연 30~40회(날짜는 ETS에서 지정)
총점	0~120점
영역별 점수	각 영역별 30점
성적 확인	응시일로부터 4~8일 후 온라인에서 성적 확인 가능

시험 영역	문제 구성	시간
Reading	● 독해 지문 2개, 총 20문제가 출제된다. ● 각 지문 길이 700단어 내외, 지문당 10개 문제	36분
Listening	● 대화(Conversation) 2개(각 5문제씩)와 강의(Lecture) 3개(각 6문제씩)가 출제된다.	36분
Break		10분
Speaking	● 독립형 과제(Independent Task) 1개, 통합형 과제(Integrated Task) 3개 총 4개 문제가 출제된다.	17분
Writing	● 통합형 과제(Integrated Task) 1개(20분) ● 수업 토론형 과제 (Writing for Academic Discussion) 1개(9분)	30분

4. iBT TOEFL®의 점수

1) 영역별 점수

Reading	0~30	Listening	0~30
Speaking	0~30	Writing	0~30

2) iBT, CBT, PBT 간 점수 비교

기존에 있던 CBT, PBT 시험은 폐지되었으며, 마지막으로 시행된 CBT, PBT 시험 이후 2년 이상이 경과되어 과거 응시자의 시험 성적 또한 유효하지 않다.

5. 시험 등록 및 응시 절차

1) 시험 등록

온라인과 전화로 시험 응시일과 각 지역의 시험장을 확인하여 신청할 수 있으며, 일반 접수는 시험 희망 응시일 7일 전까지 가능하다.

❶ 온라인 등록

ETS 토플 등록 사이트(https://www.ets.org/mytoefl)에 들어가 화면 지시에 따라 등록한다. 비용은 신용카드로 지불하게 되므로 American Express, Master Card, VISA 등 국제적으로 통용되는 신용카드를 미리 준비해 둔다. 시험을 등록하기 위해서는 회원 가입이 선행되어야 한다.

❷ 전화 등록

한국 프로메트릭 콜센터(00-7981-4203-0248)에 09:00~17:00 사이에 전화를 걸어 등록한다.

2) 추가 등록

시험 희망 응시일 3일(공휴일을 제외한 업무일 기준) 전까지 US $60의 추가 비용으로 등록 가능하다.

3) 등록 비용

2023년 현재 US $220(가격 변동이 있을 수 있음)

4) 시험 취소와 변경

ETS 토플 등록 사이트나 한국 프로메트릭(00-7981-4203-0248)으로 전화해서 시험을 취소하거나 응시 날짜를 변경할 수 있다. 등록 취소와 날짜 변경은 시험 날짜 4일 전까지 해야 한다. 날짜를 변경하려면 등록 번호와 등록 시 사용했던 성명이 필요하며 비용은 US $60이다.

5) 시험 당일 소지품

❶ 사진이 포함된 신분증(주민등록증, 운전면허증, 여권 중 하나)

❷ 시험 등록 번호(Registration Number)

6) 시험 절차

❶ 사무실에서 신분증과 등록 번호를 통해 등록을 확인한다.

❷ 기밀 서약서(Confidentiality Statement)를 작성한 후 서명한다.

❸ 소지품 검사, 사진 촬영, 음성 녹음 및 최종 신분 확인을 하고 연필과 연습장(Scratch Paper)을 제공받는다.

❹ 감독관의 지시에 따라 시험실에 입실하여 지정된 개인 부스로 이동하여 시험을 시작한다.

❺ Reading과 Listening 영역이 끝난 후 10분간의 휴식이 주어진다.

❻ 시험 진행에 문제가 있을 경우 손을 들어 감독관의 지시에 따르도록 한다.

❼ Writing 영역 답안 작성까지 모두 마치면 화면 종료 메시지를 확인한 후에 신분증을 챙겨 퇴실한다.

7) 성적 확인

응시일로부터 약 4~8일 후부터 온라인으로 점수 확인이 가능하며, 시험 전에 종이 사본 수령을 신청했을 경우 약 11-15일 후 우편으로 성적표를 받을 수 있다.

6. 실제 시험 화면 구성

TOEFL CONTINUE

General Test Information

This test measures you ability to use English in an academic context. There are 4 sections.

In the Reading section, you will answer questions to 2 reading passages.

In the Listening section, you will answer questions about 2 conversations and 3 lectures.

In the Speaking section, you will answer 4 questions. One of the questions asks you to speak about familiar topics. Other questions ask you to speak about lectures, conversations, and reading passages.

In the Writing section, you will answer 2 questions. The first question asks you to write about the relationship between a lecture you will hear and a passage you will read. The second questions asks you to write a response to an academic discussion topic.

There will be directions for each section which explain how to answer the question in that section.

Click Continue to go on.

전체 Direction

시험 전체에 대한 구성 설명

TOEFL Reading REVIEW HELP ? BACK NEXT

Question 1 of 20 00:53:28

Tundra

Tundras are areas that have long, cold winters and very short summers. The average annual temperatures of these regions are usually below zero. Because of the long cold season, the soil has a layer of permafrost, permanently frozen earth that often extends to a depth of 200 feet.
There are two types of tundra: Arctic and Alpine. Arctic tundra, found around the North Pole, is the most well known. Alpine tundra can be found at the tops of tall cold mountains, like the highest peaks in the Swiss Alps.
The plants in all tundra regions have shallow roots to allow them to grow in the shallow layer of surface soil that does thaw in summer. Animals that live in the tundra regions are also adapted to breed and raise their young quickly during the short summers.
There are two main risks to people living in tundra areas; hypothermia, the lowering of the body's core temperature, and frostbite, the constriction of blood vessels in parts of the body.

The word annual in the passage is closest in meaning to

- ○ ordinary
- ○ diurnal
- ○ conventional
- ○ yearly

Reading 영역 화면

지문은 왼쪽에, 문제는 오른쪽에 제시

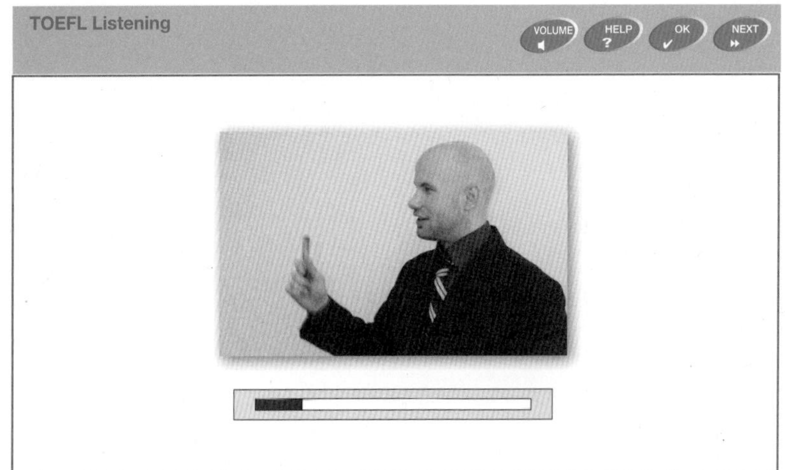

Listening 영역 화면

수험자가 대화나 강의를 듣는 동안 사진이 제시됨

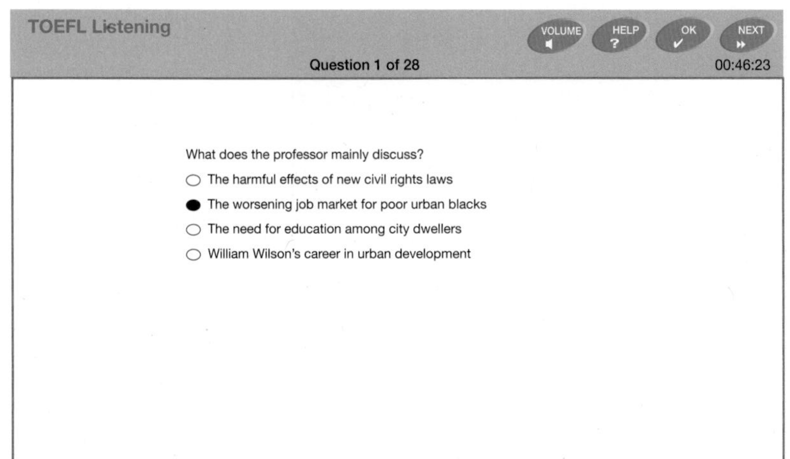

Listening 영역 화면

듣기가 끝난 후 문제 화면이 등장

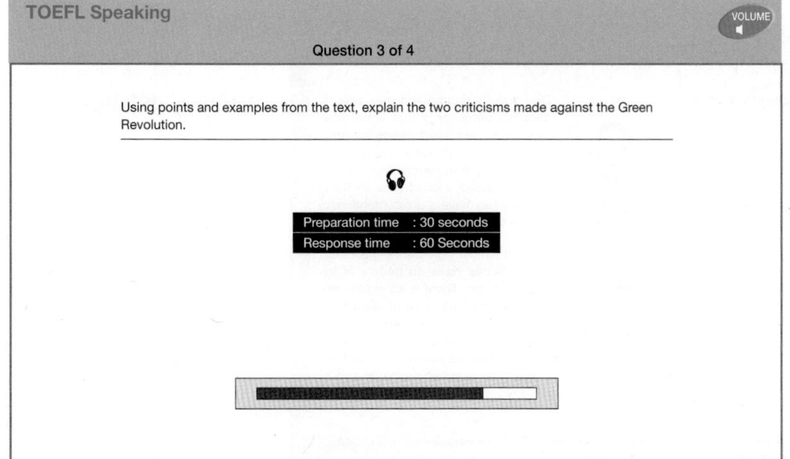

Speaking 영역 화면

문제가 주어진 후, 답변을 준비하는 시간과 말하는 시간을 알려줌

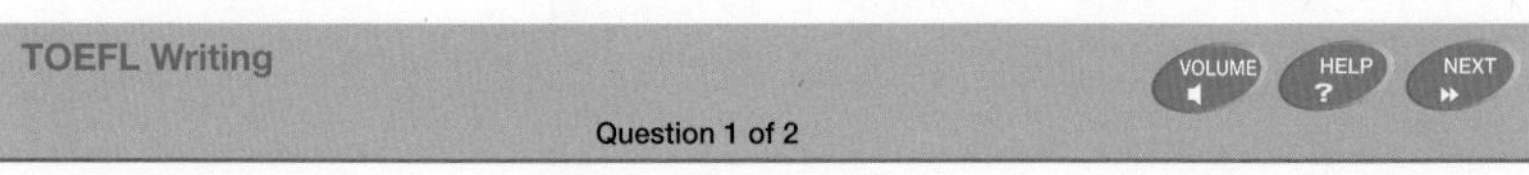

In the late 14th century, an unknown poet from the Midlands composed four poems titled *Pearl*, *Sir Gawain and the Green Knight*, *Patience*, and *Cleanness*. This collection of poems is referred to as Cotton Nero A.x and the author is often referred to as the Pearl Poet. Up to this day, there have been many theories regarding the identity of this poet, and these are three of the most popular ones.

The first theory is that the author's name was Hugh, and it is based on the *Chronicle of Andrew of Wyntoun*. In the chronicle, an author called Hucheon (little Hugh) is credited with writing three poems, one of which is about the adventures of Gawain. Not only that, but all three poems are written in alliterative verse, as are all four of the poems in *Cotton Nero A.x*. Since they are written in the same style and one poem from each set concerns Gawain, some people contend that all of the *Cotton Nero A.x* poems were written by Hugh.

The second theory is that John Massey was the poet, and it is supported by another poem called *St. Erkenwald* and penmanship. Although the actual authorship of *St. Erkenwald* is unknown, John Massey was a poet who lived in the correct area and time for scholars to attribute it to him. This manuscript was written in very similar handwriting to that of the Pearl Poet, which indicates that one person is likely the author of all five of the poems.

The third theory is that the poems were actually written by different authors from the same region of England. This comes from the fact that there is little linking the poems to each other. Two are concerned with the Arthur legends, but the only link connecting the other two is that they describe the same area of the countryside. They also seem to be written in the same dialect. Taken together, these facts indicate that they were written in the same region, but they probably were not written by the same person.

Writing 영역 화면

왼쪽에 문제가 주어지고 오른쪽에 답을 직접 타이핑할 수 있는 공간이 주어짐

복사(Copy), 자르기(Cut), 붙여넣기(Paste) 버튼이 위쪽에 위치함

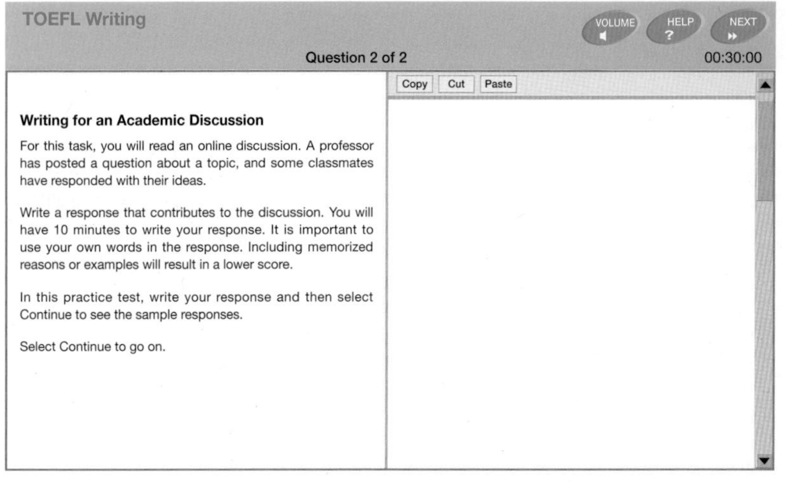

Writing 영역 화면

왼쪽에 문제가 주어지고 오른쪽에 답을 직접 타이핑할 수 있는 공간이 주어짐

복사(Copy), 자르기(Cut), 붙여넣기(Paste) 버튼이 위쪽에 위치함

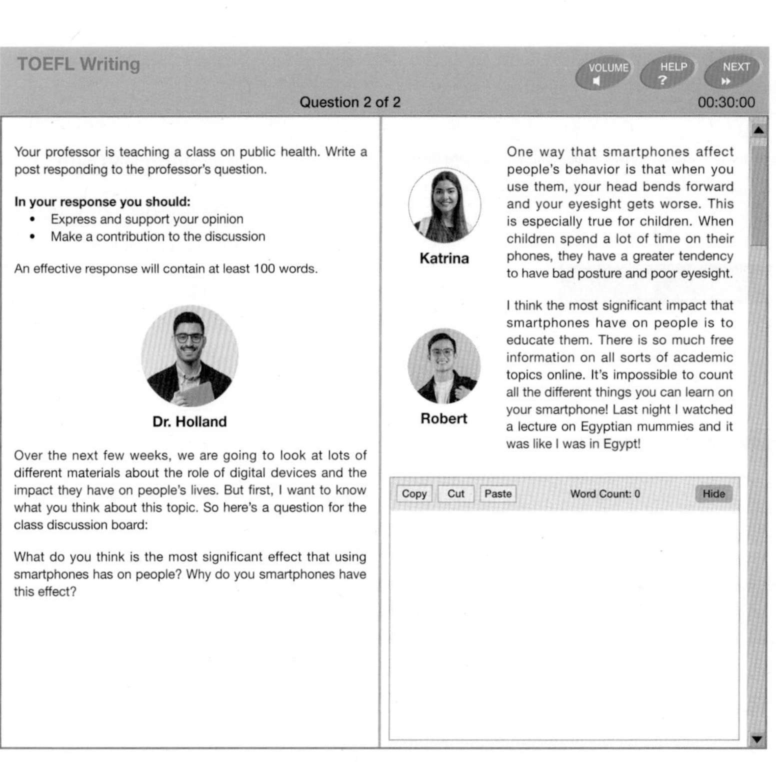

Writing 영역 화면

왼쪽에 문제가 주어지고 오른쪽에 답을 직접 타이핑할 수 있는 공간이 주어짐

복사(Copy), 자르기(Cut), 붙여넣기(Paste) 버튼이 타이핑하는 곳 위쪽에 위치함

iBT TOEFL® Writing 개요

1. Writing 영역의 특징

Writing 영역의 특징으로는 먼저 2개의 문제가 출제된다는 점을 들 수 있고, 단순히 주어진 주제에 대해 글을 쓰는 아주 기본적인 글쓰기에서 끝나는 것이 아니라, 실제 학업 상황에서 빈번하게 경험하게 되는 읽기, 듣기, 그리고 쓰기가 접목된 통합형 과제(Integrated Task)가 등장한다는 점을 그 특징으로 들 수 있다.

Writing 영역의 주요한 특징은 다음의 4가지로 정리할 수 있다.

1) Writing 영역은 2개의 문제로 구성된다.

첫 번째인 통합형(Integrated Task)은 주어진 지문(Reading Passage)을 3분간 읽고, 약 2~3분 가량의 강의자(Lecturer; Speaker)의 강의(Lecture)를 듣고 난 후, 강의자가 지문에 대해 어떤 주장을 하는지 150~225자의 단어(Words)로 20분 동안 요약(Summary)하여 글쓰기를 하는 문제다.

두 번째 문제는 2023년 7월부터 TOEFL 시험이 개정되면서 추가된 새로운 수업 토론형 과제(Writing for an Academic Discussion Task)다. 기존 독립형 과제(Independent Task)를 대체한 이 새로운 유형의 과제에서 온라인 교실 토론이 등장하는데, 다른 두 학생의 의견을 제시한 후 응시자 자신의 의견을 요구한다. 10분 동안 100자 이상의 단어로 온라인 포럼에서 댓글을 작성하듯이 자신의 의견을 표현하는 문제다.

2) 노트 필기(Note-taking)가 가능하다.

읽고, 듣고, 쓰는 문제에서 노트 필기는 매우 핵심적인 기술이다. 따라서 미리 노트 필기의 기술을 배우고 반복 연습해두어야 한다.

3) Typing만 가능하다.

수험자가 답안을 작성할 때 컴퓨터를 통한 Typing만 가능하도록 제한되어 있다. (Handwriting 불가) 미리 충분한 속도의 영타가 가능하도록 연습해야 한다. 단, Brainstorming이나 Outline은 종이에 작성할 수 있다.

4) 각 문제에 대한 평가 기준이 다르다.

Writing 영역의 핵심적인 특징 중 하나는 두 문제가 각각 다른 평가 기준(Scoring Rubric)을 가지고 있다는 점인데 고득점을 위해서는 이 평가 기준을 반드시 유념해서 답안을 작성해야 한다.

간단히 말해서 통합형 과제의 평가 기준은 내용적인 측면에 더 많은 강조를 두지만, 수업 토론형 과제의 경우 내용적인 측면과 함께 토론에 대한 연관성과 기여도에 신경을 써야 한다는 것이다.

2. Writing 영역의 문제 유형

ETS가 제시하고 있는 Writing 영역의 문제 유형은 구체적으로 다음과 같다.

1) 통합형 과제(Integrated Task)

읽기와 듣기를 기반으로 요약의 글을 완성하는 유형의 문제로서 작문 능력뿐 아니라 독해력과 청취력도 요구된다.

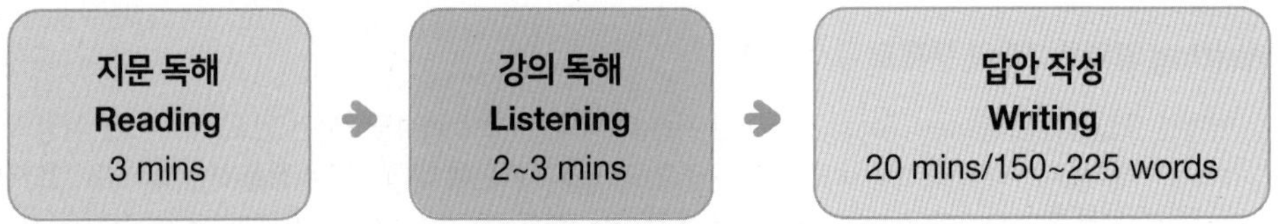

2) 수업 토론형 과제(Writing for an Academic Discussion Task)

주어진 토론 주제에 대해 두 명의 다른 학생의 의견을 읽은 후, 논리적으로 자신의 의견과 이유, 그리고 구체적인 근거를 들어 토론에 기여하는 답안을 작성하는 문제 유형이다. 따라서, 단순히 자신의 생각을 작성하는 능력뿐 아니라 다른 학생들의 의견을 파악하고 토론 주제와 관련성 있는 답변을 구사하는 능력이 요구된다.

PAGODA TOEFL

Actual Test

WRITING

PART 01
Question Types

- 01 Integrated Task
- 02 Academic Discussion Task

01 Integrated Task

- 읽기-듣기-쓰기 순으로 이어지는 통합형 과제이며, 주로 학술적인 내용을 다룬다.
- 주어진 지문을 3분간 읽고, 그 지문 내용과 관련된 약 2~3분의 강의를 듣고 난 후 강의자가 지문에 대해 어떤 주장을 하는지 150~225단어로 요약한다. 답안을 작성하는 데 총 20분의 시간이 주어진다.

문제 유형

- Summarize the points made in the lecture you just heard, explaining how they cast doubt on the points made in the reading.
  읽기 지문의 요점에 대해 어떻게 의문을 제기했는지 설명하면서 강의에서 제시한 요점을 요약하시오.

문제 풀이 전략

- 지문(reading) + 강의(listening) ···› 3가지 포인트를 잡아 요약한다.
- 지문과 강의에서 상반되는 주장이 제시되므로 이를 연결시켜 비교한다.

Reading Passage	Listening (Lecture)
Point 1	Counter point 1
Point 2	Counter point 2
Point 3	Counter point 3

- 지문과 강의가 같은 소재에 대해 언급하고 있으므로 같은 표현이 반복되기 쉽다. 이때 좋은 점수를 얻으려면 같은 단어나 표현을 반복적으로 쓰기보다는 다른 유사 단어나 표현으로 바꾸어 paraphrase하는 것이 중요하다. 따라서 동의어, 유사 표현, 비교 표현 등을 숙지할 것!

채점 기준

- 강의에서 제시된 포인트를 모두 들었는가
- 지문과 강의와의 관계를 명확하게 설명했는가
- 철자를 포함한 문법적 오류를 범하지 않았는가

핵심 유형 공략

Strategy 1 Structure

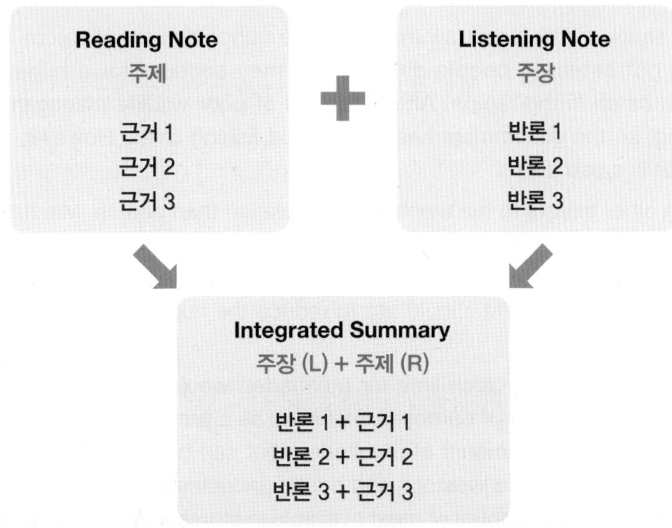

Strategy 2 Note-Taking

- 글의 주요 내용인 Main Point를 중심으로 노트 필기를 한다.

  시험 시간이 한정되어 있으므로 읽고 들은 것을 모두 적으려 하지 말고 글의 핵심 내용만 적어야 한다. 예를 들어, 연도, 퍼센트, 물량 등이 숫자로 나오면 일일이 적으려고 하지 말고 오래된 것→최근의 것, 높은 것→낮은 것, 많은 것→적은 것 등 큰 윤곽만 적도록 한다.

- 글의 구성이 파악되도록 '주제–소주제', '주제–근거'로 분류해서 노트 필기를 한다.

  읽기와 듣기는 보통 4단락으로 구성되어 있다. 각 단락의 첫 번째와 마지막 문장을 주의 깊게 보면 주제를 쉽게 파악할 수 있다. 노트 필기를 할 때, 소주제나 근거 부분은 약자나 기호를 사용하여 시간을 절약한다.

- 너무 다양한 기호를 사용하기보다는 적은 종류의 기호에 익숙해지도록 훈련하여 스스로 느낄 수 있는 부담감이나 혼동을 줄이도록 한다.

- 유용한 기호 및 약자

e.g.	for example	→	lead to, cause
etc.	et cetera, and so on	~	approximately, about
vs.	in contrast to	w/	with
cf.	compare	w/o	without
+, &	and	↔	opposite to
/	or	esp.	especially

Sample Question

TOEFL **Writing**

Question 1 of 2

Menhaden are small, oily fish that swim in massive schools in the Western Atlantic Ocean. These fish are not eaten by people directly, but they account for a huge portion of the commercial fish catch in the region. After decades of poor wildlife management, these fish are disappearing, so the government has established fishing limits. However, there are many reasons why that is a bad idea.

Firstly, there are other threats to the menhaden population than people. Menhaden have many natural predators, including striped bass, which are popular sport fish, so they have been allowed to breed unchecked. Striped bass consume huge numbers of menhaden, so they are a serious threat. The government should act to reduce the number of striped bass instead of limiting menhaden fishing.

Secondly, reducing the yearly catch limit for menhaden would affect many other industries. Their meat is used for a variety of purposes, including as a protein source in feed for livestock and poultry. If we reduce the amount of menhaden that can be caught each year, that would have an immediate effect on the livestock and poultry industries. That would affect the human food market by reducing the amount of meat available in stores and driving up prices.

Thirdly, limiting fishing of menhaden would put thousands of people out of work. About 75 percent of the menhaden catch comes from the Chesapeake Bay region, which means that most of the people involved are from the state of Virginia. The fishermen that catch the fish and the factory workers that process the fish would lose their jobs, and that would devastate the local economy.

W_01

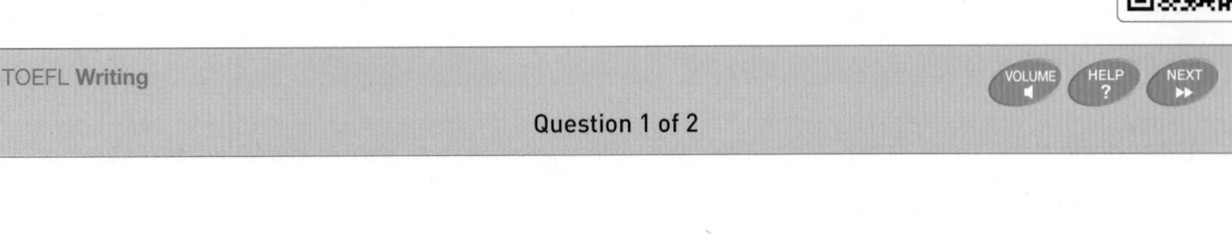
TOEFL Writing
VOLUME
HELP
?
NEXT
Question 1 of 2

Listening Note

TOEFL Writing

VOLUME HELP ? NEXT

Question 1 of 2

Directions : You have 20 minutes to plan and write your response. Your response will be judged on the basis of the quality of your writing and on how well your response presents the points in the lecture and their relationship to the reading passage. Typically, an effective response will be 150 to 225 words.

Questions : Summarize the points made in the lecture you just heard, explaining how they cast doubt on the points made in the reading.

Menhaden are small, oily fish that swim in massive schools in the Western Atlantic Ocean. These fish are not eaten by people directly, but they account for a huge portion of the commercial fish catch in the region. After decades of poor wildlife management, these fish are disappearing, so the government has established fishing limits. However, there are many reasons why that is a bad idea.

Firstly, there are other threats to the menhaden population than people. Menhaden have many natural predators, including striped bass, which are popular sport fish, so they have been allowed to breed unchecked. Striped bass consume huge numbers of menhaden, so they are a serious threat. The government should act to reduce the number of striped bass instead of limiting menhaden fishing.

Secondly, reducing the yearly catch limit for menhaden would affect many other industries. Their meat is used for a variety of purposes, including as a protein source in feed for livestock and poultry. If we reduce the amount of menhaden that can be caught each year, that would have an immediate effect on the livestock and poultry industries. That would affect the human food market by reducing the amount of meat available in stores and driving up prices.

Thirdly, limiting fishing of menhaden would put thousands of people out of work. About 75 percent of the menhaden catch comes from the Chesapeake Bay region, which means that most of the people involved are from the state of Virginia. The fishermen that catch the fish and the factory workers that process the fish would lose their jobs, and that would devastate the local economy.

문제 해설 및 스크립트

Reading Passage

청어는 서대서양에서 거대한 무리를 지어 움직이는 작고 기름기가 많은 물고기이다. 이 물고기를 사람들이 직접 먹지는 않지만, 그 지역 상업적 어획량의 큰 부분을 차지한다. 수십 년간 야생 생물에 대한 형편없는 관리가 행해진 후 이 물고기는 사라지고 있어서 정부는 어획에 제한을 두었다. 하지만 이것이 좋지 않은 생각이라는 것에는 여러 가지 이유가 있다.

첫째로, 인간보다 청어의 개체수에 위협을 주는 것들이 있다. 청어에게는 스포츠 낚시감으로 인기 있어서 억제하지 않고 사육할 수 있도록 허용되어 온 줄무늬 농어를 비롯한 많은 천적이 있다. 줄무늬 농어는 엄청난 수의 청어를 잡아먹어서 심각한 위협이 되고 있다. 정부는 청어의 어획을 제한하는 대신 줄무늬 농어의 수를 줄이기 위해 조치를 취해야 한다.

둘째로, 청어에 대한 연간 어획량을 줄이는 것은 다른 많은 산업에 영향을 줄 수 있다. 청어의 고기는 가축과 가금류를 위한 먹이에 단백질 공급원이 되는 것을 포함하여 다양한 용도로 사용된다. 만약 매년 잡을 수 있는 청어의 양을 줄인다면 즉각 축산업과 양계업에 영향을 주게 될 것이다. 이는 상점에 나오는 고기의 양이 줄어들고, 가격이 올라감으로써 우리의 식량 시장에 영향을 줄 것이다.

셋째로, 청어 어획 제한은 수많은 사람의 일자리를 잃게 할 것이다. 청어 어획의 약 75%는 체서피크만에서 나오는데, 이는 이와 연관된 대부분의 사람이 버지니아주 출신이라는 뜻이다. 청어를 잡는 어부들과 그 물고기들을 가공하는 공장 노동자들은 직업을 잃게 될 것이며, 이는 지역 경제를 파괴할 것이다.

Lecture Script

Lecturer: The population of menhaden in the Atlantic Ocean has dropped to 10 percent of what it was only decades ago, so government regulation is clearly required. In the reading, the author provides arguments against limiting the fishing of menhaden, but his reasons can easily be disproven.	**강의자:** 대서양 청어의 개체수는 몇십 년 전의 10%까지 떨어졌으며, 따라서 정부 규제가 명백히 요구됩니다. 읽기 지문에서 저자는 청어의 어획을 제한하는 것에 반대하는 주장을 제시했지만, 그의 근거는 쉽게 반증될 수 있습니다.
First, the author points out that striped bass are a natural predator of menhaden and that they eat many of the fish. He suggests reducing the number of bass to protect the menhaden, but that would be an ineffective solution. Bass eat many other fish species, so removing them would disrupt the ecosystem just as much as overfishing menhaden. Therefore, it would be much safer for the environment to reduce menhaden fishing.	첫째, 저자는 줄무늬 농어가 청어의 천적이며 많은 물고기를 잡아먹는다고 지적합니다. 그는 청어를 보호하기 위해 농어의 수를 줄이는 것을 제안했지만, 그것은 효과가 없는 해결책입니다. 농어는 많은 다른 종의 물고기들을 먹기 때문에 이들을 제거하는 것은 청어 남획만큼이나 생태계에 지장을 줄 것입니다. 그러므로 청어의 어획을 줄이는 것이 환경적으로 훨씬 더 안전합니다.
Second, the author explains that menhaden are used in many industries, especially as animal feed. While this is true, there are many other sources of protein that could be used in livestock and poultry feed instead of menhaden. One such alternative is soybeans, a crop that already has massive surpluses. Soybeans are a much more renewable resource than any kind of fish. Since they are grown on farms, they are not a part of the natural food chain and thus have little effect on the environment.	둘째, 저자는 청어가 많은 산업, 특히 가축 먹이로 사용된다고 설명합니다. 이것은 사실이지만 청어 대신 가축과 가금류의 먹이로 사용될 수 있는 다른 단백질 공급원이 많이 있습니다. 그러한 대안 중 하나가 콩인데 이것은 이미 엄청난 과잉 상태에 있는 작물입니다. 콩은 어떤 종류의 물고기보다 훨씬 더 재생 가능성이 큰 자원입니다. 콩은 농장에서 재배되기 때문에 자연적인 먹이 사슬의 일부가 아니므로 환경에 거의 영향을 주지 않습니다.

PART 01 Question Types

Third, the author states that establishing fishing limits would eliminate thousands of jobs and hurt the economy. Imposing limits would indeed affect the economy, but the effects would be temporary. The fish will reproduce and their numbers will increase. Once the fish population recovered, the fishery could be reopened with reasonable, sustainable catch limits. However, if fishermen are allowed to continue fishing without limits, they could drive the fish into extinction, and then they will have nothing to catch.	셋째, 저자는 어획량에 제한을 두는 것은 수많은 직업을 없앨 수 있고 경제를 해칠 것이라고 주장합니다. 제한을 두는 것은 실제로 경제에 영향을 줄 수 있지만, 그 영향은 한시적입니다. 물고기들은 번식할 것이고 숫자가 늘어날 것입니다. 일단 물고기 개체수가 회복되고 나면 어장은 합리적이고 지속 가능한 어획량 제한을 두고 다시 개장할 수 있을 것입니다. 하지만 만약 어부들이 제한 없이 계속해서 물고기를 잡는다면 물고기를 멸종으로 이끌게 될 것이며, 그렇게 된다면 더 잡을 것이 없어질 것입니다.

Reading Note

주제	Menhaden fish → gov't fishing limit = bad idea
근거 1	other threats = striped bass, reduce the number of them
근거 2	menhaden number down = affect other industries
근거 3	limit fishing = people will be out of work

Listening Note

주장	Menhaden fish → gov't fishing limit = bad idea → No!
반론 1	striped bass also eat many other fish species → reducing their number will disrupt ecosystem
반론 2	other alternatives can be used in place of menhaden
반론 3	the effects would be only temporary, fishery could be reopened later

Paraphrasing Practice

1	The government has established fishing limits, but there are many reasons why that is a bad idea.
	The government's policy of limiting fishing of menhaden is a bad idea, and there are several reasons that support this.

2	Bass eat many other fish species, so removing them would disrupt the ecosystem just as much as overfishing menhaden.
	Reducing the number of bass would disrupt the ecosystem, since bass are natural predators of many fish other than menhaden.

3	Since soybeans are grown on farms, they are not a part of the natural food chain and thus have little effect on the environment.
	As soybeans are grown on farms, they have little effect on the food chain, and thus are safer for the environment.

4	Limiting fishing of menhaden would put thousands of people out of work.
	Fishing limits will take jobs away from thousands of people.

Sample Summary

The reading and the lecture both talk about the government establishing fishing limits to protect menhaden and prevent them from disappearing. The reading says that limiting fishing of menhaden is a bad idea. However, the lecturer argues that the reasons suggested in the reading can easily be disproven.

Firstly, the reading says that striped bass pose a bigger threat to menhaden than fishing does, so reducing their population would be a better solution. However, the lecturer argues that this would be ineffective. Reducing the number of bass would disrupt the ecosystem, since bass are natural predators of many fish other than menhaden.

Secondly, the reading suggests that limiting fishing of menhaden will lead to a decrease in the amount of animal feed produced. The lecturer agrees that menhaden are widely used as a protein source for livestock and poultry, but also explains there are other alternatives such as soybeans. As soybeans are grown on farms, they have little effect on the food chain, and thus are safer for the environment.

Thirdly, the reading states that fishing limits will take jobs away from thousands of people involved in the fishing industry. However, the lecturer says the effects would not last long. As the fish reproduce, their population will recover. He also points out that limiting fishing would actually protect menhaden from extinction in the long run.

지문과 강의 모두 청어를 보호하고 청어가 사라지는 것을 막기 위해 정부가 어획을 제한하는 것에 대해 이야기하고 있다. 지문에서는 청어의 어획을 제한하는 것이 좋지 않은 생각이라고 말한다. 하지만 강의자는 지문에서 제시된 근거가 틀렸다는 것을 쉽게 입증할 수 있다고 주장한다.

첫째, 지문에서는 물고기를 잡는 것보다 줄무늬 농어가 청어에게 더 큰 위협을 가한다며 이들의 개체수를 줄이는 것이 더 나은 해결책일 것이라고 말한다. 하지만 강의자는 이것이 효과가 없을 것이라고 주장한다. 농어는 청어뿐만 아니라 많은 다른 물고기들의 천적이기도 하므로 농어의 수를 줄이는 것은 생태계에 지장을 줄 것이다.

둘째, 지문에서는 청어의 어획 제한이 생산되는 동물성 사료의 양을 줄어들게 할 것이라고 주장한다. 강의자는 청어가 가축과 가금류를 위한 단백질 공급원으로 널리 쓰인다는 것에 동의하면서도 콩과 같은 다른 대안이 있다고 설명한다. 콩은 농장에서 재배되기 때문에 먹이 사슬에 영향을 거의 주지 않고, 따라서 환경에 더욱 안전하다.

셋째, 지문에서는 어획 제한 때문에 어업에 관련된 수많은 사람이 직업을 잃게 될 것이라고 주장한다. 하지만 강의자는 그 영향이 오래 지속되지 않을 것이라고 말한다. 물고기가 번식함에 따라 개체수는 다시 회복될 것이다. 또한 강의자는 어획을 제한하는 것이 장기적으로 봤을 때 오히려 청어를 멸종으로부터 보호할 수 있다고 지적한다.

TOEFL Writing에서 자주 사용하는 핵심 표현들

1. 서론 문단에서 자주 사용하는 표현

지문과 강의가 의견–반박 관계일 때

In the lecture, the speaker	casts doubts on casts skepticism on expresses doubts on	~, which was explained in the reading.

강의에서 강의자는 지문에서 설명된 ~에 관해 의문을 제기하고 있다.

In the lecture, the speaker	contradicts the idea that opposes the idea that refutes the notion that challenges the idea that makes the case against	~, which was explained in the reading.

강의에서 강의자는 지문에서 설명된 ~에 대해 반박하고 있다.

EXAMPLE

- In the lecture, the speaker **casts doubts on** the point that some entertainers deserve to earn salaries in the millions, which was explained in the reading passage.
  강의에서 강의자는 읽기 지문에서 설명된 일부 연예인들이 엄청난 돈을 벌 자격이 있다는 것에 대해 의문을 제기한다.
- In the lecture, the speaker **contradicts the claim that** animal testing should not be allowed in any case, which was explained in the reading passage.
  강의에서 강의자는 읽기 지문에서 설명된 어떠한 경우에도 동물 실험이 허용되어서는 안 된다는 주장에 반박한다.
- In the lecture, the lecturer **opposes the idea that** there could be life on Mars, as mentioned in the reading passage.
  강의에서 강의자는 읽기 지문에 언급된 화성에 생물체가 있을 수 있다는 의견에 반대한다.

지문과 강의가 문제-해결책 관계일 때

In the lecture, the speaker	offers solutions for the proposes solutions for	~, which was explained in the reading.

강의에서 강의자는 지문에서 설명된 ~에 대해 해결책을 제시하고 있다.

In the lecture, the speaker	suggests alternatives for	~, which was explained in the reading.

강의에서 강의자는 지문에서 설명된 ~에 대한 대안을 제시하고 있다.

EXAMPLE

- In the lecture, the speaker **proposes solutions for** the problems caused by children's addiction to television, which was covered in the reading passage.
  강의에서 강의자는 지문에서 다루어진 아이들의 TV 중독으로 인한 문제점에 대해 해결책을 제시하고 있다.
- In the lecture, the speaker **suggests alternatives for** the problems of heavy traffic during rush hour, which was explained in the reading passage.
  강의에서 강의자는 지문에서 설명된 출퇴근 시간 동안의 교통 체증 문제에 대해 대안을 제시하고 있다.

강의의 핵심 내용에 대해 말할 때

point out	지적하다, (어떤 점을) 짚어내다
indicate	나타내다, 시사하다
stress	강조하다
explain / state	설명하다, 말하다
maintain / contend / claim / argue / assert / insist	주장하다

EXAMPLE

- The lecturer **stresses** that running your own business can also have the same problems as working for a large company.
  강의자는 자신의 사업체를 운영하는 것 또한 대기업에서 일하는 것과 똑같은 문제점을 가질 수 있다고 강조한다.
- The speaker **states** that private money and companies can support the preservation of fossils.
  강의자는 개인의 돈과 회사가 화석의 보존을 지원할 수 있다고 말한다.
- The speaker **argues** that placebos actually triggered the brain's natural painkiller.
  강의자는 위약이 실제로 뇌의 자연 진통제를 유발했다고 주장한다.

2. 본론 문단에서 자주 사용하는 표현

단락을 시작할 때

First/First of all	첫 번째로
To begin with/At the beginning	우선, 먼저
Secondly	두 번째로
Thirdly	세 번째로
In addition/Besides/Moreover/What is more	게다가, 또한
In addition to	~뿐만 아니라
Furthermore	더욱이, 더 나아가
Next	다음으로

EXAMPLE

- **First of all**, the lecturer insists that birds cannot use geographic landmarks to guide their journeys.
  첫 번째로, 강의자는 새들이 그 행로를 인도하는 데 지리적인 표지물을 사용할 수 없다고 주장한다.
- **At the beginning**, the speaker indicates that controlled decision-making is not appropriate for some decisions.
  처음에 강의자는 통제된 의사 결정은 어떤 결정에서는 적절하지 않다고 지적한다.
- **Furthermore**, the lecturer expresses doubts on the fairness of aid allocation.
  더 나아가 강의자는 원조 배당의 공평성에 대해 의문을 제기한다.
- **Next**, the lecturer argues that insects are not necessarily harmful.
  다음으로 강의자는 벌레가 반드시 해로운 것만은 아니라고 주장한다.

지문 및 강의 내용을 언급할 때

According to the reading passage[lecture]	지문[강의]에 따르면
As mentioned in the reading[lecture]	지문[강의]에서 언급된 바와 같이
In the reading[lecture]	지문[강의]에서
The reading[speaker] states/says/indicates that ~	지문[강의자]는 ~라고 말한다

EXAMPLE

- **According to the lecture**, a video is an effective teaching tool.
  강의에 따르면, 비디오는 효과적인 교육 도구이다.
- **According to the reading passage**, many new doctors start their careers in the cities because they can make more money and pay their debts off more easily.
  읽기 지문에 따르면, 많은 젊은 의사들이 더 많은 돈을 벌고 빚을 더 쉽게 갚을 수 있기 때문에 도시에서 일을 시작한다.
- **The speaker indicates that** older employees often feel isolated and decide to quit as their colleagues are replaced by younger employees.
  강의자는 나이가 든 직장인들은 종종 고립되어 있다고 느끼고, 동료들이 더 젊은 인력들로 대체되면 그만두기로 결정한다고 지적한다.

앞에서 말한 것과 반대되는 내용을 언급할 때

However, the lecturer explains that ~	하지만 강의자는 ~라고 설명한다
On the other hand	반면에, 다른 한편으로는
On the contrary	그와는 반대로
Nevertheless	그럼에도 불구하고
In contrast to ~	~와는 대조적으로

EXAMPLE

- **However, the speaker states that** textbooks are much more reliable and cost-effective.
  하지만 강의자는 교과서가 훨씬 더 믿을 만하고 비용 면에서 효과가 크다고 말한다.

- **On the contrary**, the speaker indicates that removing dead trees takes away many nutrients from the surrounding soil.
  반대로 강의자는 죽은 나무를 제거하는 것은 주변의 토양으로부터 많은 영양분을 빼앗는다고 지적한다.

- **In contrast**, the lecturer argues that grading class participation will result in poorer quality of classes.
  반대로 강의자는 수업 참여도를 점수 매기는 것은 질적으로 더 낮은 수업을 초래할 것이라고 주장한다.

의미의 흐름을 정리 혹은 강조할 때; 뜸들일 때

In fact	사실은, 실제로
Well, actually	음, 사실은
Um…	음…
This clearly shows/illustrates that ~	이것은 ~을 명확히 보여준다/설명한다

EXAMPLE

- **In fact**, learning a new language can improve memory and problem-solving skills.
  실제로 새로운 언어를 배우는 것이 기억력과 문제 해결 능력을 향상시킬 수 있다.

- **Well, actually**, I don't think that's entirely true.
  음, 사실은 나는 그게 완전히 사실이라고 생각하지 않는다.

- **This clearly shows that** regular exercise is essential for maintaining good health.
  이것은 규칙적인 운동이 건강을 유지하는 데 필수적이라는 것을 명확히 보여준다.

02 Academic Discussion Task

- Academic Discussion Task는 TOEFL Writing 시험의 두 번째 과제로, 온라인 학술 토론 형식을 기반으로 한다.
- 시험에서는 교수가 제시한 질문과 두 명의 학생이 이에 대한 의견을 게시한 토론 게시판이 주어진다.
- 학문적 주제에 대해 자신의 의견을 논리적으로 표현하고 토론에 기여하는 것이 목적이며, 자신의 의견을 최소 100단어 이상으로 작성해야 한다. 주어진 시간은 10분이다.

문제 유형

- **선택형(Choice Type)**
  Which is more important in learning — curiosity or discipline?
  학습에서 호기심과 규율 중 어느 것이 더 중요한가요?
- **장점/단점형(Advantage/Disadvantage Type)**
  What is one advantage or disadvantage of taking online classes?
  온라인 수업을 듣는 것의 장점과 단점은 무엇인가요?
- **우선순위형(Priority/Importance Type)**
  Which invention has had the greatest impact besides computers and smartphones?
  컴퓨터와 스마트폰 외에 가장 큰 영향을 끼친 발명품은 무엇인가요?
- **해결책 제시형(Solution Type)**
  How can universities reduce stress for students?
  대학은 학생들의 스트레스를 어떻게 줄일 수 있을까요?
- **동의/반대형(Agree/Disagree Type)**
  Do you agree with Lena's idea? Why or why not?
  레나의 생각에 동의하시나요? 왜 그런가요? 혹은 왜 그렇지 않은가요?

문제 풀이 전략

- 교수자의 질문과 학생들의 응답을 주의 깊게 읽어 전체 맥락을 파악한다. 교수의 질문을 통해 키워드와 목적을 파악하고, 학생 A, B의 의견을 통해 어떤 입장인지 파악(동의/반대, 예시, 이유 등)한다.
- 주어진 논의에 대해 동의하거나 새로운 관점을 제시할 주제를 선택한다. 다른 학생과 같은 관점 또는 다른 관점을 선택하고, 자신만의 이유와 예시 1~2개를 준비한다.
- 서론, 본론, 결론의 구조를 유지하며, 각 부분에서 자신의 의견과 그에 대한 근거를 제시한다. '도입 → 이유 1 → 이유 2 → 결론' 구조로 간단명료하게 작성한다.
- 10분이라는 제한된 시간 내에 답변을 완성하고, 검토할 시간을 확보한다. 1분 남기고 문법, 철자, 표현 오류를 확인한다.

채점 기준

- 아이디어가 주제와 관련 있고, 충분한 설명과 예시로 뒷받침된 의견인가
- 다양한 문장 구조와 어휘를 자연스럽게 사용했는가
- 어휘 선택이 적절하고 문법, 철자, 구두점 사용 등의 오류가 최소한인가

핵심 유형 공략

Strategy 1 Structure

도입 (1~2문장)	• 교수의 질문에 대한 자신의 의견 제시 • 학생 A 또는 B의 의견 언급 여부 선택 (동의/반대)
본론 (3~4문장)	• 이유 1 + 설명/예시 • 이유 2 + 설명/예시
결론 (1문장)	• 핵심 주장 재확인 또는 한 문장 요약

• 보통 본론은 두 가지를 제시하지만, 시간이 충분하고 근거를 더 대고 싶다면 세 번째 본론을 덧붙여도 좋다.

Strategy 2 선택형 (Choice Type)

한쪽을 명확히 선택하고, 구체적인 이유나 예시를 제시한다.

e.g. **Learning – Curiosity vs. Discipline**

Q Which is more important in learning – curiosity or discipline?

A I believe discipline is more important. Discipline 규율 선택 Curiosity is helpful, but without discipline, students may not follow through with their studies. For example, preparing for an exam takes focus and daily effort. Even when the topic is boring, discipline helps students keep going and succeed. 규율을 선택한 이유/예시 제시

Strategy 3 장단점형 (Advantage/Disadvantage Type)

장점이나 단점 중 하나에 집중하고, 예시를 포함한다.

e.g. **Online vs. In-person Classes**

Q What is one advantage of online classes?

A One big advantage of online classes is flexibility. Students can study at any time and from any place. This is especially useful for people who work or live far from school. 온라인 수업의 장점 설명 I took an online English course last year, and it helped me improve without quitting my part-time job. 장점에 대한 본인의 경험 제시

Strategy 4 우선순위형 (Priority/Importance Type)

우선순위/중요성을 강조하고 비교 또는 영향력 중심으로 설명한다.

e.g. **Invention**

Ⓠ What is one important invention besides computers and smartphones?

Ⓐ I think the Internet is one of the most important inventions. 컴퓨터와 스마트폰 외에 '인터넷'을 중요한 발명이라고 밝힘 It allows people to access unlimited information and communicate instantly across the world. For example, students can take online classes and learn from international professors. 인터넷의 중요성과 예시 제시 This invention has completely changed how we live, work, and study. 인터넷의 중요성을 한 번 더 강조

PART 01 Question Types

Strategy 5 해결책 제시형 (Solution Type)

구체적이고 실현 가능한 아이디어를 제시한다.

e.g. **Stress in University**

Ⓠ How can universities reduce stress for students?

Ⓐ Universities can reduce stress by offering more mental health support. 질문의 표현을 사용하여 해결책 제시 Many students feel pressure from exams and job searches. If schools provide counseling and stress management workshops, students can feel more relaxed and perform better in their studies. 해결책을 제시한 근거와 구체적인 적용 방법을 기술

Strategy 6 동의/반대형 (Agree/Disagree Type)

학생의 의견 인용 후 동의/반대 및 이유를 설명한다.

e.g. **Working While Studying**

Ⓠ Do you agree or disagree with the idea that students should work part-time while studying?

Ⓐ I agree with Paul that students should work part-time while studying. 학업 중 아르바이트를 해야 한다는 학생의 의견에 동의 Part-time jobs help students learn time management and earn money. I worked at a café during university, and it taught me responsibility. However, the job should not interfere with study time. 동의하는 이유와 예시 제시

Sample Question 1 선택형 (Choice Type)

TOEFL Writing

Question 2 of 2

Your professor is teaching a class on education and personal development. Write a post responding to the professor's question.

In your response, you should:
- Express and support your opinion
- Make a contribution to the discussion

An effective response will contain at least 100 words. You have 10 minutes to write it.

Dr. Albert

Today, we're going to examine a classic debate in education and personal development—whether success in life depends more on natural talent or on hard work and persistence. Both have their supporters. Talent can offer a head start, but consistent effort may yield more reliable results over time. In your opinion, which one contributes more to achieving long-term success, and why?

Paul

I believe talent plays a more significant role in achieving success. While hard work is definitely important, some individuals are born with abilities that simply can't be taught. Whether it's musical ability, mathematical thinking, or athletic coordination, those with natural gifts often reach higher levels faster and with less effort. Even with years of training, others may struggle to match that level of performance.

Lena

I would argue that hard work is ultimately more important than talent. Talent might help at the beginning, but it can only take someone so far. Success usually requires consistent practice, discipline, and perseverance. Someone who is determined and puts in the effort every day can improve gradually and even surpass someone who was initially more talented but less dedicated.

Sample Answer

I agree with Lena that hard work is more important than talent in achieving lasting success. While natural ability can offer an advantage at the beginning, it doesn't guarantee long-term achievement.

Introduction Hard work matters more than talent.

First, hard work helps people build skills over time. For example, someone who practices the piano every day can outperform a naturally gifted player who only practices occasionally. Second, working hard builds resilience and discipline, which are critical for overcoming challenges. Talented people may give up when they face obstacles, but hard-working individuals are more likely to persist.

Body Effort builds skills and helps overcome obstacles.

Therefore, in most situations, I believe effort and consistency matter more than innate ability.

Conclusion Persistence and consistency lead to success.

알버트 교수: 오늘 수업에서는 교육과 개인의 성장에 있어 중요한 고전적인 논쟁을 살펴보겠습니다. 바로 인생의 성공이 타고난 재능에 더 의존하는가, 아니면 노력과 끈기에 더 의존하는가에 대한 주제입니다. 두 관점 모두 지지자들이 있습니다. 재능은 빠른 시작을 가능하게 할 수 있지만, 지속적인 노력은 시간이 지남에 따라 더 안정적인 결과를 가져올 수 있습니다. 여러분의 의견은 어떻습니까? 장기적인 성공을 이루는 데 있어서 어느 쪽이 더 중요한 역할을 한다고 생각하나요?

폴: 저는 성공을 이루는 데 있어 재능이 더 중요한 역할을 한다고 생각합니다. 물론 노력이 중요하다는 점은 인정하지만, 일부 사람들은 단순히 타고난 능력을 지니고 있습니다. 예를 들어, 음악적 재능, 수학적 사고력, 운동 능력 등은 배워서 익히기 어려운 경우가 많습니다. 이런 재능을 가진 사람들은 훈련을 많이 하지 않아도 더 빨리 높은 수준에 도달할 수 있습니다. 반면, 다른 사람들은 수년간 훈련을 해도 그 수준에 도달하기 어려울 수 있습니다.

레나: 저는 결국에는 노력하는 것이 재능보다 더 중요하다고 생각합니다. 재능은 초기에는 도움이 되지만, 그 자체만으로는 한계가 있습니다. 성공을 이루기 위해서는 꾸준한 연습과 규칙적인 습관, 인내심이 필수입니다. 매일 노력하는 사람은 점차 발전할 수 있고, 처음에는 더 뛰어난 재능을 가진 사람보다 더 나은 결과를 낼 수도 있습니다. 결국, 지속적인 노력이 성공으로 가는 핵심 열쇠라고 생각합니다.

샘플 답변: 저는 레나의 의견에 동의합니다. 인생에서 성공을 이루는 데는 타고난 재능보다 꾸준한 노력과 끈기가 더 중요하다고 생각합니다. 선천적인 능력은 시작할 때는 유리할 수 있지만, 그것만으로는 오랜 기간의 성취를 보장할 수 없습니다.
첫째, 노력은 시간이 지날수록 기술을 발전시킵니다. 예를 들어, 매일 피아노 연습을 하는 사람은, 가끔 연습하는 재능 있는 사람보다 더 뛰어난 연주자가 될 수 있습니다. 둘째, 노력은 인내심과 자기 통제를 기르게 하며, 이는 어려움을 극복하는 데 꼭 필요한 요소입니다. 재능 있는 사람들은 좌절할 때 쉽게 포기할 수 있지만, 노력하는 사람은 계속 도전합니다.
따라서 대부분은 타고난 재능보다는 꾸준함과 노력이 더 중요하다고 생각합니다.

Sample Question 2 장단점형 (Advantage/Disadvantage Type)

TOEFL Writing

Question 2 of 2

Your professor is teaching a class on global education. Write a post responding to the professor's question.

In your response, you should:

- Express and support your opinion
- Make a contribution to the discussion

An effective response will contain at least 100 words. You have 10 minutes to write it.

Dr. Albert

Let's discuss the experience of studying in a foreign country. Many students choose to go abroad for their education, hoping for personal and academic growth. However, this choice also comes with potential challenges, including financial costs and cultural adjustment. In your opinion, what is one significant advantage or disadvantage of studying abroad, and how does it impact students?

Paul

One major advantage of studying abroad is that it exposes students to new cultures and perspectives. Living in a different country helps people understand the world better, improve their language skills, and become more independent. These experiences can be very helpful both personally and professionally. I think it's one of the best ways to grow.

Lena

While studying abroad sounds exciting, I think the financial burden is a serious disadvantage. Tuition fees and living expenses can be much higher than studying at home. Some students even take out large loans or work part-time, which can affect their focus on studies. It might not be worth the cost for everyone.

Sample Answer

I think one of the greatest advantages of studying abroad is the opportunity for cultural immersion and personal development.

Students who live in another country gain a deeper understanding of global issues, interact with diverse groups of people, and become more adaptable. For instance, a friend of mine studied in Germany and returned with better language skills, stronger confidence, and international job offers. These benefits wouldn't have been possible through domestic study alone. Although it can be expensive, the long-term rewards—such as career growth, language proficiency, and global awareness—can outweigh the initial cost.

Therefore, I believe the advantages of studying abroad make it a worthwhile investment.

Introduction Studying abroad offers personal and cultural benefits.

Body It improves adaptability, language skills, and career opportunities.

Conclusion The advantages make studying abroad a worthwhile investment.

알버트 교수: 외국에서 공부하는 경험에 관해 이야기해 봅시다. 많은 학생이 개인적, 학문적 성장을 기대하며 유학을 선택합니다. 하지만, 이 선택에는 재정적 부담이나 문화적 적응 같은 어려움도 따를 수 있습니다. 여러분의 생각에는, 유학의 중요한 장점 또는 단점 중 하나는 무엇이며, 그것이 학생들에게 어떤 영향을 미친다고 생각하나요?

폴: 유학의 큰 장점 중 하나는 학생들이 새로운 문화와 다양한 시각을 경험할 수 있다는 점입니다. 다른 나라에서 생활하면서 사람들은 세상을 더 넓게 이해하고, 언어 능력을 향상하며, 더 독립적인 성향을 보이게 됩니다. 이런 경험은 개인적인 면에서도, 직업적인 면에서도 매우 도움이 됩니다. 저는 유학이 성장할 수 있는 최고의 방법의 하나라고 생각합니다.

레나: 유학은 흥미로워 보일 수 있지만, 재정적 부담이 매우 큰 단점이라고 생각합니다. 수업료와 생활비는 국내에서 공부할 때보다 훨씬 더 비쌀 수 있습니다. 어떤 학생들은 큰 대출을 받거나 아르바이트하기도 하는데, 이는 학업에 집중하는 데 방해가 될 수 있습니다. 모든 학생에게 유학이 항상 그만한 가치가 있는 것은 아닐 수 있습니다.

샘플 답변: 제가 생각하기에 유학의 큰 장점 중 하나는 문화 체험과 개인적 성장을 할 수 있다는 점입니다.
다른 나라에서 생활하는 학생들은 다양한 문화와 사람들을 직접 경험하며 세계에 대한 이해도가 깊어집니다. 예를 들어, 제 친구는 독일에서 유학했는데, 영어 실력은 물론 자신감도 높아졌고, 국제 기업에서 일할 기회도 얻었습니다. 이러한 혜택은 국내에서 공부하는 것만으로는 얻기 어려운 것들입니다. 물론 비용이 많이 들 수는 있지만, 경력 성장, 언어 능력 향상, 글로벌 감각이라는 장기적인 보상을 생각하면 그만한 가치는 충분합니다.
그래서 저는 유학이 투자할 만한 가치가 있는 경험이라고 믿습니다.

Sample Question 3 우선순위형 (Priority/Importance Type)

TOEFL Writing

Your professor is teaching a class on the history of technology. Write a post responding to the professor's question.

In your response, you should:

- Express and support your opinion
- Make a contribution to the discussion

An effective response will contain at least 100 words. You have 10 minutes to write it.

Dr. Albert

Throughout history, many inventions have changed the way we live, work, and communicate. While computers and smartphones are often mentioned, there are many other innovations that have had a major impact on modern life. Think about inventions in areas such as transportation, communication, or science. What do you think is one of the most important inventions in modern history, other than the computer and the smartphone?

Paul

I would say that electricity is the most important invention. Without it, none of our modern technologies would work. Lights, refrigerators, internet, medical equipment—everything depends on electricity. It's the foundation for our modern way of life and enabled the development of many other important tools and machines we use today.

Lena

I believe the Internet is the invention that has had the biggest impact on modern life. It completely changed how we connect, learn, and work. People can take online courses, run businesses, and talk to others across the world in real time. The Internet has made the world smaller and more efficient.

Sample Answer

I agree with Lena that the Internet is one of the most transformative inventions in modern history.

While electricity made it possible, the Internet redefined how we access information and connect with others. It enables online learning, remote work, instant communication, and global commerce. For example, in Korea, many small businesses now thrive through online platforms, and students attend virtual classes using mobile devices. It also plays a vital role in healthcare, allowing professionals to share data and research worldwide.

Because of its influence on nearly every aspect of daily life, including education, business, and social interaction, I believe the Internet has had the most profound impact of any recent invention.

Introduction The Internet is the most important modern invention.

Body It changed communication, education, business, and healthcare.

Conclusion The Internet's influence is greater than any other.

알버트 교수: 역사 속에서 많은 발명품들이 우리의 생활, 업무, 소통 방식을 변화시켜 왔습니다. 컴퓨터나 스마트폰처럼 자주 언급되는 것들도 있지만, 그 외에도 현대 생활에 큰 영향을 미친 여러 혁신이 존재합니다. 교통, 통신, 과학 분야에서 발명품들을 떠올려 보세요. 여러분이 생각하기에 컴퓨터와 스마트폰을 제외하고, 현대 역사에서 가장 중요한 발명품은 무엇이며 그 이유는 무엇인가요?

폴: 저는 전기가 가장 중요한 발명품이라고 생각합니다. 전기가 없다면 오늘날 우리가 사용하는 어떤 기술도 작동하지 않을 것입니다. 전등, 냉장고, 인터넷, 의료 기기 등 모든 것이 전기에 의존합니다. 전기는 현대 생활 방식의 기초가 되었고, 우리가 현재 사용하는 다양한 도구와 기계를 발전할 수 있게 했습니다.

레나: 저는 인터넷이 현대 생활에 가장 큰 영향을 준 발명품이라고 생각합니다. 인터넷은 우리가 서로 연결하고, 배우고, 일하는 방식을 완전히 바꾸어 놓았습니다. 사람들은 온라인 강의를 듣고, 사업을 운영하며, 세계 어디에 있는 사람과도 실시간으로 대화할 수 있게 되었습니다. 인터넷은 세상을 더 작고 효율적으로 만들었습니다.

샘플 답변: 저는 레나의 의견에 동의합니다. 인터넷은 현대 역사에서 가장 혁신적인 발명 중 하나라고 생각합니다.
전기가 인터넷의 기반이 되긴 했지만, 인터넷은 정보 접근 방식과 인간의 소통 방식을 완전히 바꿔 놓았습니다. 온라인 학습, 원격 근무, 즉각적인 의사소통, 글로벌 상거래 등 모든 것이 가능해졌습니다. 예를 들어, 한국에서는 많은 소상공인들이 온라인 플랫폼을 통해 성공을 이루었고, 학생들은 스마트 기기로 원격 수업을 듣고 있습니다. 또한, 의료 분야에서도 전문가들이 데이터를 공유하고 협력할 수 있게 되었습니다.
이처럼 교육, 비즈니스, 사회생활 등 삶의 거의 모든 부분에 영향을 미쳤기 때문에 인터넷은 현대 사회에서 가장 중요한 발명이라고 생각합니다.

Sample Question 4 해결책 제시형 (Solution Type)

TOEFL Writing

Question 2 of 2

Your professor is teaching a class on student wellness and academic success. Write a post responding to the professor's question.

In your response, you should:

- Express and support your opinion
- Make a contribution to the discussion

An effective response will contain at least 100 words. You have 10 minutes to write it.

Dr. Albert

Many university students report feeling overwhelmed by stress, especially due to academic pressure, competition, and future uncertainty. This kind of stress can negatively affect both mental health and academic performance. What is one effective way that universities can help students reduce stress and create a healthier learning environment?

Paul

I think universities should offer more opportunities for students to join clubs or take part in sports and social events. These activities help students relax, make friends, and feel part of a community. That kind of social connection can reduce stress and improve mental health.

Lena

I believe universities should reduce the number of major exams or space them out better throughout the semester. When all the big tests are scheduled together, students feel a lot of pressure. Better planning and flexibility could help lower student stress levels.

Sample Answer

I think the most effective way for universities to reduce stress among students is by providing accessible mental health resources.

Introduction Mental health support is the best way to reduce stress.

While social activities and flexible exams are helpful, professional support can address deeper emotional issues. For instance, schools could offer free counseling services, peer support groups, and stress-relief workshops on campus. In Korea, many students experience intense academic pressure, but they hesitate to seek help due to stigma. If universities normalize mental health support and make it easy to access, students would feel more comfortable getting assistance.

Body Counseling and peer programs help students cope better.

This approach not only supports individual well-being but also helps students stay focused and succeed academically.

Conclusion Supporting mental well-being improves academic performance.

알버트 교수: 많은 대학생이 학업 스트레스, 경쟁, 미래에 대한 불확실성 등으로 인해 압박감을 심하게 느낀다고 보고하고 있습니다. 이러한 스트레스는 정신 건강과 학업 성과 모두에 부정적인 영향을 미칠 수 있습니다. 대학이 학생들의 스트레스를 줄이고 더 건강한 학습 환경을 조성하기 위해 할 수 있는 효과적인 방법은 무엇이라고 생각하나요?

폴: 저는 대학이 학생들이 동아리 활동에 참여하거나 스포츠, 사교 행사에 참여할 기회를 더 많이 제공해야 한다고 생각합니다. 이러한 활동은 학생들이 긴장을 풀고, 친구를 사귀고, 소속감을 느끼는 데 도움이 됩니다. 이런 사회적 연결은 스트레스를 줄이고 정신 건강을 향상하는 데 큰 역할을 합니다.

레나: 저는 대학이 중간 및 기말고사와 같은 큰 시험의 개수를 줄이거나, 학기 전반에 더 고르게 배치해야 한다고 생각합니다. 모든 중요한 시험이 몰려 있으면, 학생들은 큰 압박을 느낍니다. 시험 일정을 더 잘 계획하고 유연하게 운영한다면, 학생들의 스트레스 수준을 줄이는 데 도움이 될 수 있다고 생각합니다.

샘플 답변: 저는 대학이 학생들의 스트레스를 줄이기 위해 가장 효과적으로 할 수 있는 방법은 접근할 수 있는 정신 건강 지원을 제공하는 것으로 생각합니다.
동아리 활동이나 시험 일정 조정도 도움이 되지만, 전문가의 도움은 더 깊은 감정 문제를 해결할 수 있습니다. 예를 들어, 학교는 무료 상담 서비스, 또래 상담 그룹, 스트레스 해소 워크숍 등을 제공할 수 있습니다. 한국에서는 많은 학생들이 높은 학업 스트레스를 받지만, 사회적 낙인이나 정보 부족 때문에 도움을 요청하지 못하는 경우가 많습니다. 만약 학교에서 정신 건강 지원을 정상화하고 쉽게 이용할 수 있게 한다면, 많은 학생이 편안하게 도움을 받을 수 있을 것입니다.
이러한 접근은 학생 개인의 복지를 도울 뿐만 아니라 학업 성공에도 긍정적인 영향을 줄 것입니다.

Sample Question 5 동의/반대형 (Agree/Disagree Type)

TOEFL Writing

Question 2 of 2

Your professor is teaching a class on time management and student life. Write a post responding to the professor's question.

In your response, you should:

- Express and support your opinion
- Make a contribution to the discussion

An effective response will contain at least 100 words. You have 10 minutes to write it.

Dr. Albert

Many students take part-time jobs during their studies. Some educators believe that working while studying helps students develop real-world skills and responsibility. Others argue that it distracts students from academics and increases stress. Based on your experience or observations, do you agree or disagree with the idea that part-time jobs benefit students?

Paul

I support the idea of part-time jobs for students. They learn time management, communication, and work ethic. I worked part-time in a bookstore and learned to handle customers, solve problems, and balance my schedule. It helped me grow as a person.

Lena

I disagree. I think students already have too much academic pressure. A part-time job just adds more stress. I've seen friends get sick or fall behind in school because they were working too much. For most students, focusing on school is more important.

Sample Answer

I agree with Paul that part-time jobs can be very beneficial for students.

They teach practical skills like time management, teamwork, and communication. When I worked part-time as a barista, I learned how to deal with difficult customers, meet deadlines, and handle responsibilities. These skills helped me later during internships and group projects. Also, part-time jobs help students become more independent and confident.

Of course, it's important to maintain a healthy balance, but if managed well, working part-time can offer valuable life lessons that go beyond what we learn in the classroom.

Introduction Part-time jobs are beneficial for student growth.

Body They teach real-life skills like time management and responsibility.

Conclusion When balanced well, part-time jobs offer lifelong value.

알버트 교수: 많은 학생이 학업과 함께 아르바이트하고 있습니다. 몇몇 교육자들은 일을 하면서 공부하는 것이 실제 사회에서 필요한 기술과 책임감을 기르는 데 도움이 된다고 주장합니다. 반면에, 다른 사람들은 아르바이트가 학업에 방해가 되고 스트레스를 증가시킨다고 말합니다. 여러분의 경험이나 관찰을 바탕으로, 아르바이트가 학생들에게 도움이 된다고 생각하나요? 아니면 그렇지 않다고 생각하나요?

폴: 저는 학생들이 아르바이트하는 것에 찬성합니다. 아르바이트를 통해 학생들은 시간 관리, 의사소통 능력, 직업 윤리와 같은 중요한 기술을 배울 수 있습니다. 저도 서점에서 아르바이트했던 경험이 있는데, 그때 고객을 응대하고 문제를 해결하며 일정을 조율하는 방법을 배웠습니다. 이런 경험들은 제 개인적인 성장에 큰 도움이 되었습니다.

레나: 저는 반대하는 견해입니다. 요즘 학생들은 이미 학업 스트레스가 너무 많습니다. 아르바이트는 단지 그 스트레스를 더 늘릴 뿐입니다. 제 친구 중에는 일 때문에 아프거나 학업이 뒤처진 예도 있었습니다. 대부분의 학생에게는 학업에 집중하는 것이 더 중요하다고 생각합니다.

샘플 답변: 저는 폴의 의견에 동의합니다. 아르바이트는 학생들에게 매우 유익할 수 있다고 생각합니다.
아르바이트는 시간 관리, 협업, 의사소통 같은 실용적인 기술을 길러 줍니다. 저는 고등학교 시절 카페에서 일하면서 까다로운 손님을 응대하고 마감 시간에 맞춰 일하며 책임감을 배웠습니다. 이러한 경험은 이후 인턴십이나 조별 과제에도 큰 도움이 되었습니다. 또한, 아르바이트는 학생들이 더 독립적이고 자신감 있게 성장하도록 도와줍니다.
물론 학업과의 균형이 중요하지만, 잘 조절한다면 아르바이트는 교실에서 배울 수 없는 소중한 삶의 교훈을 줄 수 있습니다.

TOEFL Writing에서 자주 사용하는 핵심 표현들

1. 서론 문단에서 자주 사용되는 표현

서론은 보통 1~2문장으로 구성하며, 질문에 대한 자신의 의견을 명확히 밝혀야 한다. 토론의 주제를 직접 언급하고 논지를 간단히 제시하여 본론으로 자연스럽게 연결한다.

V 의견 제시

I believe that …	저는 …라고 생각합니다
In my opinion, …	제 의견으로는 …
I agree/disagree that …	저는 …에 동의/반대합니다
From my perspective	제 관점에서 …

V 토론 맥락 언급

Regarding the topic of …	…에 대한 주제에 관하여
In response to the professor's question about …	교수님의 …에 대한 질문에 답하여
Considering the discussion on …	…에 대한 논의를 고려할 때

V 논지 간단 소개

I strongly support the idea that …	저는 …라는 아이디어를 강력히 지지합니다
I am inclined to argue that …	저는 …라고 주장하고 싶습니다
It seems to me that …	…라고 생각됩니다

EXAMPLE

- **In response to the professor's question about** online education, **I strongly support the idea that** it is as effective as in-person learning.
  교수님의 온라인 교육에 대한 질문에 대해, 저는 그것이 대면 수업만큼 효과적이라는 의견에 강하게 동의합니다.

사용 팁

- 서론은 20~30단어로 짧게 유지하여 본론에 충분한 분량을 할애한다.
- 격식 있는 표현을 사용하고, 축약형을 피한다. (I'm 대신 I am으로 쓰기)
- 질문에 직접 답하여 토론에 참여하는 모습을 보여준다.

2. 본론 문단에서 자주 사용되는 표현

본론은 자신의 의견을 1~2개의 이유, 예시, 설명으로 뒷받침하는 핵심 파트이다. 학술적이면서도 대화적인 톤으로, 선택한 학생의 의견에 간단히 반응하며 자신의 주장을 강화해야 하며, 단락 하나를 길게 쓰거나 두 개로 나눠서 쓴다.

V 이유 소개

One reason for my view is that …	제 의견의 한 가지 이유는 …입니다
Firstly, I believe that …	우선 저는 …라고 생각합니다
To begin with …	우선, …

V 예시 제공

For example, …	예를 들어, …
To illustrate, …	이를 보여주는 사례로, …
A clear instance of this is …	이에 대한 명확한 예시는 …입니다

V 인과 설명

As a result, …	그 결과, …
This leads to …	이것은 …로 이어집니다
Consequently, …	따라서, …

V 다른 의견에 반응

While A argues that …, I believe …	A는 …라고 주장하지만, 저는 …라고 생각합니다
I agree with B that …, but I would add …	B가 …라고 한 점에 동의하지만, …을 덧붙이고 싶습니다
In contrast to A's point, I think …	A의 주장과 달리, 저는 …라고 생각합니다

V 추가 이유 제시

Additionally, …	또한, …
Another reason is that …	또 다른 이유는 …입니다
Furthermore, …	게다가, …

EXAMPLE

- **One reason for my view is that** online education allows flexible learning schedules. **For example,** students can access recorded lectures anytime, which is especially helpful for those who have part-time jobs or family responsibilities.

  제 의견의 한 가지 이유는 온라인 교육이 유연한 학습 일정을 가능하게 한다는 점입니다. 예를 들어, 학생들은 녹화된 강의를 언제든지 시청할 수 있어, 아르바이트를 하거나 가족을 돌봐야 하는 학생들에게 특히 유용합니다.

- **Additionally,** online tools enhance collaboration. To illustrate, platforms like Zoom enable group discussions.

  또한, 온라인 도구는 협업을 향상시킵니다. 이를 보여주는 사례로, Zoom 같은 플랫폼은 그룹 토론을 가능하게 합니다.

- **While A argues that** online learning lacks interaction, **I believe that** virtual breakout rooms effectively address this concern by allowing students to engage in smaller, focused conversations.

  A는 온라인 학습이 상호작용이 부족하다고 주장하지만, 저는 가상 토론방이 학생들이 더 작고 집중적인 대화를 나눌 수 있도록 해 줌으로써 이 문제를 효과적으로 해결한다고 생각합니다.

사용 팁

- 본론은 70~100단어로 권장 분량을 채운다.
- 구체적인 예시로 설득력을 높인다.
- 연결어(예: For example)를 반복하지 않고 다양화한다.
- 다른 학생의 의견을 언급할 때는 간단히 다루어 자신의 주장에 집중한다.

3. 결론 문단에서 자주 사용되는 표현

결론은 의견을 재확인하고 주요 요점을 요약하거나 최종 생각을 남기는 파트로, 1~2문장으로 간결하게 마무리한다. 새로운 아이디어를 추가하지 않도록 주의한다.

V 의견 재확인

In conclusion, I believe that …	결론적으로, 저는 …라고 생각합니다
To sum up, I maintain that …	요약하자면, 저는 …를 유지합니다
Overall, it is clear that …	전반적으로, …가 분명합니다

V 주요 요점 요약

Given these reasons, …	이러한 이유로, …
Based on the points discussed, …	논의한 바를 바탕으로, …
Considering the above, …	위 내용을 고려할 때, …

V 최종 생각 남기기

Thus, I encourage further discussion on …	따라서, …에 대한 추가 논의를 권장합니다
This suggests that …	이는 …를 시사합니다
Ultimately, this highlights the importance of …	궁극적으로, 이는 …의 중요성을 강조합니다

EXAMPLE

- **In conclusion, I believe that** online education is effective due to its flexibility and tools.

  결론적으로, 저는 유연성과 도구 때문에 온라인 교육이 효과적이라고 생각합니다.

사용 팁

- 결론은 15~25단어로 간결하게 유지한다.
- 본론의 세부사항을 그대로 반복하지 말고, 의견을 다르게 표현한다.
- 확신 있는 톤으로 강한 인상을 남긴다.

PART 02
Actual Tests

Actual Test 01

Actual Test 02

Actual Test 03

Actual Test 04

Actual Test 05

Actual Test 06

Actual Test 07

문제 듣기

Actual Test 01

예시 답변 및 해석 | p. 2

TOEFL Writing

Question 1 of 2

Due to their higher level of energy efficiency, many governments are advocating the use of compact fluorescent lamps (CFLs). While they may be superior to regular incandescent bulbs in many respects, research suggests that they are not the wonder solution that so many people seem to think they are.

Firstly, just like any other type of fluorescent lamp, CFLs contain mercury. They may last a long time, but eventually they must be replaced, and mercury is highly toxic. If they are put in landfills, the mercury could leak out into the water table and rivers, poisoning the fish and people. The mercury is also a hazard for people who work in recycling plants because the bulbs are easily broken.

Secondly, CFLs are pretty expensive. Depending on the size and wattage, they can cost 3 to 10 times as much as the bulbs they are meant to replace. These prices are unlikely to go down for some time as the technology is still being refined. Unless the government intends to mandate lower prices for the lamps, it would put a financial burden on consumers, especially on companies in large buildings.

Finally, although they produce light more efficiently, the quality of that light is lower. Brighter lamps are a good thing, but the chemicals these lights use produce a much narrower spectrum of visible light. This harsher light is likely to irritate people who are using them; just as conventional fluorescent bulbs often give people sore eyes and headaches.

AT01

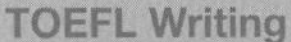

TOEFL Writing

Question 1 of 2

TOEFL Writing

Directions : You have 20 minutes to plan and write your response. Your response will be judged on the basis of the quality of your writing and on how well your response presents the points in the lecture and their relationship to the reading passage. Typically, an effective response will be 150 to 225 words.

Questions : Summarize the points made in the lecture you just heard, explaining how they cast doubt on the points made in the reading.

Due to their higher level of energy efficiency, many governments are advocating the use of compact fluorescent lamps (CFLs). While they may be superior to regular incandescent bulbs in many respects, research suggests that they are not the wonder solution that so many people seem to think they are.

Firstly, just like any other type of fluorescent lamp, CFLs contain mercury. They may last a long time, but eventually they must be replaced, and mercury is highly toxic. If they are put in landfills, the mercury could leak out into the water table and rivers, poisoning the fish and people. The mercury is also a hazard for people who work in recycling plants because the bulbs are easily broken.

Secondly, CFLs are pretty expensive. Depending on the size and wattage, they can cost 3 to 10 times as much as the bulbs they are meant to replace. These prices are unlikely to go down for some time as the technology is still being refined. Unless the government intends to mandate lower prices for the lamps, it would put a financial burden on consumers, especially on companies in large buildings.

Finally, although they produce light more efficiently, the quality of that light is lower. Brighter lamps are a good thing, but the chemicals these lights use produce a much narrower spectrum of visible light. This harsher light is likely to irritate people who are using them; just as conventional fluorescent bulbs often give people sore eyes and headaches.

TOEFL Writing

Your professor is teaching a class. Write a post responding to the professor's question.

In your response, you should:

- express and support your opinion
- make a contribution to the discussion

An effective response will contain at least 100 words.
You will have 10 minutes to write it.

Dr. Robert

Some people believe that universities are justified in investing in sports activities, while others argue that education should be prioritized. Which position do you agree with?

Paul

I personally believe that sports programs should receive equal funding to education. Plato argued that both physical development and intellectual development are essential to success. Investing in sports only furthers the idea that a healthy mind should exist in balance with a healthy body. I also believe that sports teams are a great venue for students to take part in healthy competition, finding unity in their school colors, but also being driven to excel.

Rebecca

My opinion leans toward more emphasis on education. A university is a place of learning. If, as Paul is implying, it is a place for sports as well, then every university student should be on a sports team. Sports do not equate to physical education; I believe such education takes place in actual classes that teach sports and physical skills, and for which the student receives credits. Thus, in line with the distinction I am trying to make, investing in facilities for better physical education classes would make more sense than funding competitive athletic programs that the vast majority of students cannot participate in, beyond being spectators.

Copy | Cut | Paste   Word Count: 0   Hide

문제 듣기

Actual Test 02

예시 답변 및 해석 | p. 7

TOEFL Writing

Question 1 of 2

Of all the sharks that swim in the oceans, none has such a distinct profile as the hammerhead shark. The hammer-shaped elongated head for which it is named makes it instantly recognizable, and it has invited speculation for centuries. Obviously, such a radical alteration in shape must be an adaptation, but for what purpose?

Due to the shape of their heads and their relatively small mouths, some have proposed that the hammer-shaped head is used as a weapon. Hammerheads typically hunt near the sea floor, and they could use their head to strike prey, slamming it into the ground. Indeed, some hammerheads have been observed holding their prey down while they devour it. A more normally shaped head would make this tactic difficult if not impossible to carry out.

The wide flat shape of the head may serve another physical purpose, which is acting as a kind of hydrofoil. Other species of shark are dedicated to moving in more or less a straight line once they begin a strike. However, hammerheads have been observed rapidly changing direction, and their head could be the reason. Much like the wings of an airplane, the head shape could provide lift in the water. This additional energy could easily be channeled into making sharper turns while pursuing prey.

The hammer shape may also serve the purpose of increasing their sensory ability. Like most species of shark, hammerheads have electro-sensory organs located on the underside of their snouts. These sensitive organs allow them to detect the faint electrical signals that all animals emit, allowing the sharks to track their prey more easily. The increased number of sensory organs would compensate for the limited field of vision their eye placement would cause.

AT02

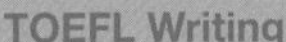

Question 1 of 2

TOEFL Writing

VOLUME HELP ? NEXT

Question 1 of 2

Directions : You have 20 minutes to plan and write your response. Your response will be judged on the basis of the quality of your writing and on how well your response presents the points in the lecture and their relationship to the reading passage. Typically, an effective response will be 150 to 225 words.

Questions : Summarize the points made in the lecture you just heard, explaining how they cast doubt on the points made in the reading.

Of all the sharks that swim in the oceans, none has such a distinct profile as the hammerhead shark. The hammer-shaped elongated head for which it is named makes it instantly recognizable, and it has invited speculation for centuries. Obviously, such a radical alteration in shape must be an adaptation, but for what purpose?

Due to the shape of their heads and their relatively small mouths, some have proposed that the hammer-shaped head is used as a weapon. Hammerheads typically hunt near the sea floor, and they could use their head to strike prey, slamming it into the ground. Indeed, some hammerheads have been observed holding their prey down while they devour it. A more normally shaped head would make this tactic difficult if not impossible to carry out.

The wide flat shape of the head may serve another physical purpose, which is acting as a kind of hydrofoil. Other species of shark are dedicated to moving in more or less a straight line once they begin a strike. However, hammerheads have been observed rapidly changing direction, and their head could be the reason. Much like the wings of an airplane, the head shape could provide lift in the water. This additional energy could easily be channeled into making sharper turns while pursuing prey.

The hammer shape may also serve the purpose of increasing their sensory ability. Like most species of shark, hammerheads have electro-sensory organs located on the underside of their snouts. These sensitive organs allow them to detect the faint electrical signals that all animals emit, allowing the sharks to track their prey more easily. The increased number of sensory organs would compensate for the limited field of vision their eye placement would cause.

Copy | Cut | Paste | Undo | Redo | Hide Word Count | 0

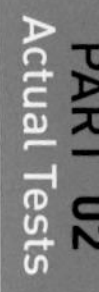

TOEFL Writing

Your professor is teaching a class. Write a post responding to the professor's question.

In your response, you should:

- express and support your opinion
- make a contribution to the discussion

An effective response will contain at least 100 words.
You will have 10 minutes to write it.

Dr. Jay

Nowadays, there is a lot of emphasis put on honesty. Our interpersonal communications textbook is no exception. It also stresses the need for communicators to speak truthfully and honestly. It argues that honesty builds trust, encourages cooperation, and strengthens bonds. But do you think this is always the case? Do you agree or disagree that there are situations in which telling a lie is better than telling the truth?

Paul

I believe it's best to hold fast to what our textbook teaches. Think about situations where we consider telling a small, seemingly harmless lie. Let's say you're a mother who was diagnosed with a serious illness. Many would consider lying to their children to protect them from the truth. Can you imagine how hurt the children would feel when they find out the truth? Instead of protecting them, you've hurt those closest to you. Instead, just as our textbook says, being honest is the right way. It can bring the family closer together, helping them cherish their time more and face the challenges ahead.

Rebecca

I agree with Paul. In my personal experience, I can't tell you how many times I've been able to fix a problem simply by telling the truth. This has been the case specifically in situations where I considered withholding the truth. I simply can't operate when there is a lie that I need to maintain. Whenever I withhold information from someone, nothing is ever the same. I become someone else, and I need to constantly work to continue as if the lie were true. In the end, I do a disservice to myself, to those around me, and to the potential for a great future.

Copy Cut Paste Word Count: 0 Hide

문제 듣기

Actual Test 03

예시 답변 및 해석 | p. 13

TOEFL Writing

Question 1 of 2

An increasing number of companies have either adopted or are in the midst of considering the positive effects of a four-day workweek. Proponents of this policy argue that this would lead to greater gains for both employees as well as companies.

First, a shorter workweek can significantly enhance an employee's work-life balance. Burnout is becoming too common a problem these days. Shorter workweeks would allow workers to allocate more time to personal pursuits, hobbies, and family responsibilities, leading to improved mental health and overall well-being. With more time for rest and relaxation, employees are likely to return to work rejuvenated, keeping them happy.

In addition, research suggests that shorter workweeks can lead to increased productivity and efficiency. By compressing work into fewer days, employees are often more focused and motivated to complete tasks within a shorter timeframe. This can result in reduced procrastination, fewer distractions, and higher levels of concentration during work hours. Moreover, as mentioned, an extra day off leaves employees with the opportunity to recharge, further resulting in higher-quality output.

Finally, offering flexible work arrangements such as a four-day workweek can make companies more attractive to prospective employees and enhance employee retention. In a competitive job market, organizations that prioritize employee well-being and offer innovative work arrangements are more likely to attract top talent. Additionally, employees who feel valued and supported by their employers are less likely to seek employment elsewhere, reducing turnover costs and fostering a more stable workforce.

AT03

TOEFL Writing

Question 1 of 2

TOEFL Writing

Question 1 of 2

Directions : You have 20 minutes to plan and write your response. Your response will be judged on the basis of the quality of your writing and on how well your response presents the points in the lecture and their relationship to the reading passage. Typically, an effective response will be 150 to 225 words.

Questions : Summarize the points made in the lecture you just heard, explaining how they cast doubt on the points made in the reading.

An increasing number of companies have either adopted or are in the midst of considering the positive effects of a four-day workweek. Proponents of this policy argue that this would lead to greater gains for both employees as well as companies.

First, a shorter workweek can significantly enhance an employee's work-life balance. Burnout is becoming too common a problem these days. Shorter workweeks would allow workers to allocate more time to personal pursuits, hobbies, and family responsibilities, leading to improved mental health and overall well-being. With more time for rest and relaxation, employees are likely to return to work rejuvenated, keeping them happy.

In addition, research suggests that shorter workweeks can lead to increased productivity and efficiency. By compressing work into fewer days, employees are often more focused and motivated to complete tasks within a shorter timeframe. This can result in reduced procrastination, fewer distractions, and higher levels of concentration during work hours. Moreover, as mentioned, an extra day off leaves employees with the opportunity to recharge, further resulting in higher-quality output.

Finally, offering flexible work arrangements such as a four-day workweek can make companies more attractive to prospective employees and enhance employee retention. In a competitive job market, organizations that prioritize employee well-being and offer innovative work arrangements are more likely to attract top talent. Additionally, employees who feel valued and supported by their employers are less likely to seek employment elsewhere, reducing turnover costs and fostering a more stable workforce.

TOEFL Writing

Your professor is teaching a class. Write a post responding to the professor's question.

In your response, you should:

- express and support your opinion
- make a contribution to the discussion

An effective response will contain at least 100 words.
You will have 10 minutes to write it.

Dr. Bobby

Some people believe that maintaining strong relationships with existing friends and colleagues is more beneficial than meeting new people. Do you agree or disagree?

Ben

In my case, I happen to see more merit in expanding my network. I hate to say it, but we live in a world where we must recognize that we capitalize on everything, even our relationships. What can they bring to the table? How can I get back what I invest in someone else? What benefits does this person bring to my life? I don't think this can be helped, nor do I think it's morally wrong. The more we expand our network, the more we are able to expect returns. More connections mean more people to turn to when we need something. You simply have a greater chance of success the more relationships you forge.

Suzan

I happen to agree with Ben, that capitalizing on relationships is completely natural in today's world. However, I also believe that capitalizing on relationships works better if your relationships are of better quality. Say you operate like Ben, and you know hundreds of people at a shallow level. If one of them is a professor who, for example, could write a recommendation letter for your first-choice graduate school program, and you want to capitalize on that relationship, it's going to take more than just a few cursory greetings here and there to have an effect on your chances of getting into the program. It's going to take a deeper relationship than that. This is why I think everyone should focus on quality rather than quantity when it comes to human relationships.

Copy | Cut | Paste | Word Count: 0 | Hide

문제 듣기

Actual Test 04

예시 답변 및 해석 | p. 19

TOEFL Writing

Question 1 of 2

In areas that often suffer from drought or severe storms, people sometimes use cloud seeding in order to increase or alter the precipitation they receive. Typically, silver iodide or dry ice is dropped into clouds, lowering their internal temperatures. The usefulness of this practice has been proven in many areas.

In laboratory experiments, scientists created ideal conditions for hail formation and dispersed silver iodide into the clouds. The resultant precipitation was comparatively harmless snow as opposed to hailstones. This means that cloud seeding can be used both to limit the extent of damaging weather like hail as well as to promote snow or rainfall for beneficial reasons. In addition, this proves that the principle behind the idea of cloud seeding is sound.

North American scientists have proven the effectiveness of cloud seeding in the real world as well. One of the main threats to crops in the American Midwest is hail damage. Scientists flew airplanes into clouds that had the potential for creating hail and released chemicals. As a result, the clouds only dropped rain. Not only that, but the US government experimented with using silver iodide to weaken hurricanes. After releasing canisters of silver iodide into the eye wall of a hurricane, they observed a 10% drop in wind speeds.

Outside confirmation of the practical uses of cloud seeding has come from many other countries, including China. The Chinese regularly use the same techniques to prevent hail over cities as well as farms. In addition, they have even used cloud seeding to cause beneficial precipitation when there was none to be had. In 1997, they were suffering from a prolonged drought, so scientists seeded clouds and created a heavy snowfall.

AT04

Question 1 of 2

TOEFL Writing

Directions : You have 20 minutes to plan and write your response. Your response will be judged on the basis of the quality of your writing and on how well your response presents the points in the lecture and their relationship to the reading passage. Typically, an effective response will be 150 to 225 words.

Questions : Summarize the points made in the lecture you just heard, explaining how they cast doubt on the points made in the reading.

In areas that often suffer from drought or severe storms, people sometimes use cloud seeding in order to increase or alter the precipitation they receive. Typically, silver iodide or dry ice is dropped into clouds, lowering their internal temperatures. The usefulness of this practice has been proven in many areas.

In laboratory experiments, scientists created ideal conditions for hail formation and dispersed silver iodide into the clouds. The resultant precipitation was comparatively harmless snow as opposed to hailstones. This means that cloud seeding can be used both to limit the extent of damaging weather like hail as well as to promote snow or rainfall for beneficial reasons. In addition, this proves that the principle behind the idea of cloud seeding is sound.

North American scientists have proven the effectiveness of cloud seeding in the real world as well. One of the main threats to crops in the American Midwest is hail damage. Scientists flew airplanes into clouds that had the potential for creating hail and released chemicals. As a result, the clouds only dropped rain. Not only that, but the US government experimented with using silver iodide to weaken hurricanes. After releasing canisters of silver iodide into the eye wall of a hurricane, they observed a 10% drop in wind speeds.

Outside confirmation of the practical uses of cloud seeding has come from many other countries, including China. The Chinese regularly use the same techniques to prevent hail over cities as well as farms. In addition, they have even used cloud seeding to cause beneficial precipitation when there was none to be had. In 1997, they were suffering from a prolonged drought, so scientists seeded clouds and created a heavy snowfall.

Your professor is teaching a class. Write a post responding to the professor's question.

In your response, you should:

- express and support your opinion
- make a contribution to the discussion

An effective response will contain at least 100 words.
You will have 10 minutes to write it.

Dr. Albert

Next week, we'll be discussing the various ways AI development could shape society, both positively and negatively. Before we dive into that in class, I'd like to get your input on this. I have an inquiry for the message board: "Should AI be heavily regulated, or should there be minimal restrictions?"

Jane

We need very strong regulations on artificial intelligence to mitigate potential risks. While AI can help solve complex problems, the possible harms it could cause, such as job displacement due to automation, are too significant to overlook. There are also ethical concerns, such as the misuse of data and violations of privacy, that need to be addressed. Without proper oversight, AI could create more harm than good. Therefore, I believe regulating AI will ensure that its development remains ethical and responsible, preventing societal disruption while still allowing for innovation in a controlled and thoughtful manner.

Mark

I think overregulating artificial intelligence could stifle its potential for groundbreaking advancements. Therefore, minimal regulation would benefit society the most. While there are risks, such as job displacement and ethical concerns as Jane mentioned, AI also has immense potential to address critical challenges in fields like medicine, climate change, and space exploration. Instead of restricting its development, we should focus on ensuring responsible use of AI through guidelines and best practices. The true value of AI lies in how it is applied, and with the right approach, it can become a powerful tool for solving problems that humanity cannot tackle alone.

Copy | Cut | Paste | Word Count: 0 | Hide

문제 듣기

Actual Test 05

예시 답변 및 해석 | p. 25

TOEFL Writing

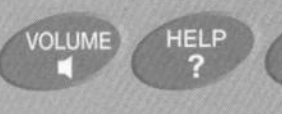

Question 1 of 2

In order to attract qualified teachers, schools in many poor and rural areas offer signing bonuses. These financial incentives are a vital investment in the future of students, and as such should be continued.

The main issue that schools in low-income areas face is attracting teachers to work at them. Public schools are funded by state income tax revenue, which means that their budgets are determined by the average income in their area. Therefore, the pay for teachers in poor areas is typically low, which makes it difficult to attract new teachers. So, by providing higher incomes, signing bonuses allow these schools to attract teachers that would otherwise teach in higher income areas.

The increased salaries that signing bonuses create also attract people from other industries. Many people who are interested in teaching choose not to due to the low average salary that teaching offers. Instead, they pursue other careers in their area of study. For example, scientists working for private corporations can make far more money than they would by teaching science to students. Higher wages can attract these experts to lower income schools in their area where they would not normally consider working.

Signing bonuses are also beneficial because they encourage teachers to remain at one institution for a longer period of time. Most of the institutions stipulate that the teacher must teach for a specific number of years in order to receive their bonus. Many also divide the bonus up between the stipulated years in order to motivate the teacher to stay longer. This allows the schools to retain their teachers longer, and provides a stable environment for their students.

TOEFL Writing

Question 1 of 2

Directions : You have 20 minutes to plan and write your response. Your response will be judged on the basis of the quality of your writing and on how well your response presents the points in the lecture and their relationship to the reading passage. Typically, an effective response will be 150 to 225 words.

Questions : Summarize the points made in the lecture you just heard, explaining how they cast doubt on the points made in the reading.

In order to attract qualified teachers, schools in many poor and rural areas offer signing bonuses. These financial incentives are a vital investment in the future of students, and as such should be continued.

The main issue that schools in low-income areas face is attracting teachers to work at them. Public schools are funded by state income tax revenue, which means that their budgets are determined by the average income in their area. Therefore, the pay for teachers in poor areas is typically low, which makes it difficult to attract new teachers. So, by providing higher incomes, signing bonuses allow these schools to attract teachers that would otherwise teach in higher income areas.

The increased salaries that signing bonuses create also attract people from other industries. Many people who are interested in teaching choose not to due to the low average salary that teaching offers. Instead, they pursue other careers in their area of study. For example, scientists working for private corporations can make far more money than they would by teaching science to students. Higher wages can attract these experts to lower income schools in their area where they would not normally consider working.

Signing bonuses are also beneficial because they encourage teachers to remain at one institution for a longer period of time. Most of the institutions stipulate that the teacher must teach for a specific number of years in order to receive their bonus. Many also divide the bonus up between the stipulated years in order to motivate the teacher to stay longer. This allows the schools to retain their teachers longer, and provides a stable environment for their students.

TOEFL Writing

Your professor is teaching a class. Write a post responding to the professor's question.

In your response, you should:

- express and support your opinion
- make a contribution to the discussion

An effective response will contain at least 100 words.
You will have 10 minutes to write it.

Dr. Emily

In our recent classes, we've been discussing the use of weight-loss drugs. There is a significant debate about their role. Some people see these drugs as a quick fix to a complicated problem, while others argue they can provide the necessary support for people struggling with weight-related health issues. Would you support weight-loss drugs or lifestyle changes?

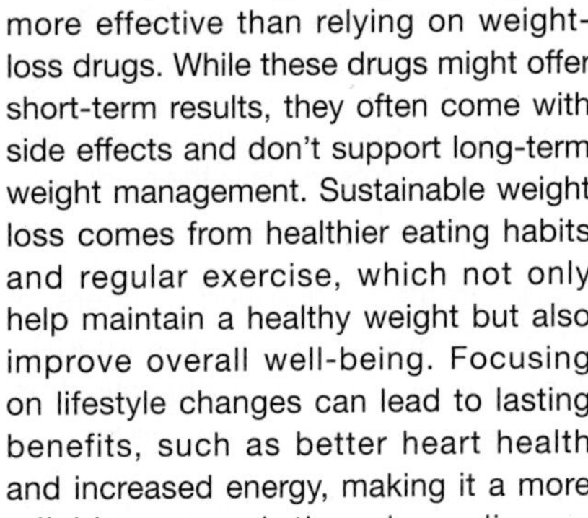

Jaslene

I believe promoting lifestyle changes is more effective than relying on weight-loss drugs. While these drugs might offer short-term results, they often come with side effects and don't support long-term weight management. Sustainable weight loss comes from healthier eating habits and regular exercise, which not only help maintain a healthy weight but also improve overall well-being. Focusing on lifestyle changes can lead to lasting benefits, such as better heart health and increased energy, making it a more reliable approach than depending on medication alone.

Alexander

While I agree with Jaslene's point that lifestyle changes are important, I think weight-loss drugs can play a helpful role for certain individuals. For example, some people face genetic or medical challenges that make losing weight difficult, even with diet and exercise. In these cases, weight-loss drugs can offer valuable support. Rather than dismissing their use, I believe they can be part of a comprehensive approach to weight management, particularly for those who struggle with conventional methods. In the end, isn't it better to help people actually lose weight and maintain it through drugs rather than watch them fail using methods that don't work for them?

Copy | Cut | Paste | Word Count: 0 | Hide

문제 듣기

Actual Test 06

예시 답변 및 해석 | p. 31

TOEFL Writing

Question 1 of 2

Historically, the British Isles were invaded by many foreign forces such as the Celts, the Romans, and the Angles and Saxons. In light of this history, it is easy to see why it is unclear whom the people of England are descended from. However, there is strong evidence that points to the Anglo-Saxons as the ancestors of the majority of modern English people.

To begin with, historical records show that the movement of the Anglo-Saxons to the British Isles was a resettlement. They left their former homes on the mainland in what is now Germany and Denmark and came to England, which was inhabited by Celtic tribes. Written accounts from around that time give the impression that this wave of immigration quickly overwhelmed the Celts and forced them to retreat into what is now Wales and Scotland.

This is further supported by the fact that English developed from the language of the Anglo-Saxons and not the earlier Celts. A simple comparison of English with Welsh or Gaelic, both Celtic tongues, clearly shows how drastically different these languages are. As the Anglo-Saxons exerted their dominance over the island, their language replaced those of the Celtic peoples. This linguistic shift increases the likelihood that today's population came from the Germanic invaders.

Even more conclusive proof was gained by studying the DNA of people living in several villages in eastern England. Their DNA was compared to samples from modern people with Celtic and Germanic backgrounds, and it was found to be almost identical to that of people living in the areas where the Anglo-Saxon migration began. This provides inarguable proof that the people of modern-day England are more closely related to the Anglo-Saxons than to the original Celtic population.

AT06

TOEFL Writing

Question 1 of 2

Directions : You have 20 minutes to plan and write your response. Your response will be judged on the basis of the quality of your writing and on how well your response presents the points in the lecture and their relationship to the reading passage. Typically, an effective response will be 150 to 225 words.

Questions : Summarize the points made in the lecture you just heard, explaining how they cast doubt on the points made in the reading.

Historically, the British Isles were invaded by many foreign forces such as the Celts, the Romans, and the Angles and Saxons. In light of this history, it is easy to see why it is unclear whom the people of England are descended from. However, there is strong evidence that points to the Anglo-Saxons as the ancestors of the majority of modern English people.

To begin with, historical records show that the movement of the Anglo-Saxons to the British Isles was a resettlement. They left their former homes on the mainland in what is now Germany and Denmark and came to England, which was inhabited by Celtic tribes. Written accounts from around that time give the impression that this wave of immigration quickly overwhelmed the Celts and forced them to retreat into what is now Wales and Scotland.

This is further supported by the fact that English developed from the language of the Anglo-Saxons and not the earlier Celts. A simple comparison of English with Welsh or Gaelic, both Celtic tongues, clearly shows how drastically different these languages are. As the Anglo-Saxons exerted their dominance over the island, their language replaced those of the Celtic peoples. This linguistic shift increases the likelihood that today's population came from the Germanic invaders.

Even more conclusive proof was gained by studying the DNA of people living in several villages in eastern England. Their DNA was compared to samples from modern people with Celtic and Germanic backgrounds, and it was found to be almost identical to that of people living in the areas where the Anglo-Saxon migration began. This provides inarguable proof that the people of moden-day England are more closely related to the Anglo-Saxons than to the original Celtic population.

TOEFL Writing

Question 2 of 2

Your professor is teaching a class. Write a post responding to the professor's question.

In your response, you should:

- express and support your opinion
- make a contribution to the discussion

An effective response will contain at least 100 words.
You will have 10 minutes to write it.

Dr. Noah

Some people think that governments should provide financial support to encourage higher birth rates, while others believe that social policies, such as better childcare and parental leave, are more effective. What are your thoughts on this?

Eva

In my opinion, investing in better childcare facilities would be the most effective strategy to boost birth rates. The high cost and limited availability of quality childcare are significant concerns for many potential parents. By providing affordable, high-quality childcare options, we could make it easier for people to balance work and family life. This support would relieve some of the financial pressure and make parenthood more accessible to a broader range of people, potentially encouraging more families to have children and contributing to increased birth rates.

John

I agree with Eva that having better childcare facilities might be helpful for many parents. However, I believe providing generous maternity and paternity leave would be the best way to boost birth rates. A well-structured parental leave policy would give parents the necessary time to bond with their newborns without worrying about their job security or financial stability. This would make parenthood more attractive to many people, as they wouldn't feel pressured to immediately return to work. Also, giving parents the time and support they need during the early stages of parenthood could make the idea of having children more appealing.

Copy | Cut | Paste | Word Count: 0 | Hide

PART 02
Actual Tests

문제 듣기

Actual Test 07

예시 답변 및 해석 | p. 37

TOEFL Writing

Question 1 of 2

The technology of genetic modification offers many potential advances, especially in agriculture. The creation of genetically modified organisms (GMOs) is a revolution in science that may allow us to grow sufficient food and even improve a country's economy in the following ways.

First, GMOs can resolve one of the most significant difficulties many farmers face: a lack of precipitation. By genetically modifying crops to grow in dry conditions, science could give these farmers a higher yield from their land. If they can grow enough to have a surplus, they can sell the extra at the market. In this way, not only the farmers, but also the local and even the national economy could benefit.

Second, another threat that farmers face is pest organisms, particularly insects and fungi. However, GMOs can be created that produce toxins that will protect them against pests and remain harmless to people. With such crops, synthetic pesticides would be unnecessary, which benefits not only consumers, but also the environment. Chemical pesticides are a serious environmental pollutant, and they can affect many species other than the ones they are intended to kill.

Third, GMO crops can provide a variety of nutrients for many people who suffer from malnutrition due to their limited diet. These people suffer from vitamin deficiencies that can severely affect their health. However, these GMO crops are able to combat this situation because they can provide nutrients that the plants normally would not contain. For example, many cultures use rice as their staple crop, but it lacks vitamin A, which is required to grow properly. So, scientists have created a type of rice that contains large amounts of vitamin A to supplement their diet.

AT07

Question 1 of 2

TOEFL Writing

Question 1 of 2

Directions : You have 20 minutes to plan and write your response. Your response will be judged on the basis of the quality of your writing and on how well your response presents the points in the lecture and their relationship to the reading passage. Typically, an effective response will be 150 to 225 words.

Questions : Summarize the points made in the lecture you just heard, explaining how they cast doubt on the points made in the reading.

The technology of genetic modification offers many potential advances, especially in agriculture. The creation of genetically modified organisms (GMOs) is a revolution in science that may allow us to grow sufficient food and even improve a country's economy in the following ways.

First, GMOs can resolve one of the most significant difficulties many farmers face: a lack of precipitation. By genetically modifying crops to grow in dry conditions, science could give these farmers a higher yield from their land. If they can grow enough to have a surplus, they can sell the extra at the market. In this way, not only the farmers, but also the local and even the national economy could benefit.

Second, another threat that farmers face is pest organisms, particularly insects and fungi. However, GMOs can be created that produce toxins that will protect them against pests and remain harmless to people. With such crops, synthetic pesticides would be unnecessary, which benefits not only consumers, but also the environment. Chemical pesticides are a serious environmental pollutant, and they can affect many species other than the ones they are intended to kill.

Third, GMO crops can provide a variety of nutrients for many people who suffer from malnutrition due to their limited diet. These people suffer from vitamin deficiencies that can severely affect their health. However, these GMO crops are able to combat this situation because they can provide nutrients that the plants normally would not contain. For example, many cultures use rice as their staple crop, but it lacks vitamin A, which is required to grow properly. So, scientists have created a type of rice that contains large amounts of vitamin A to supplement their diet.

TOEFL Writing

Your professor is teaching a class. Write a post responding to the professor's question.

In your response, you should:

- express and support your opinion
- make a contribution to the discussion

An effective response will contain at least 100 words.
You will have 10 minutes to write it.

Dr. Janet

Our class has been examining the ethical implications of consuming and farming animals. Some argue that human consumption necessitates a degree of animal farming, while others advocate for a shift to plant-based diets for ethical and environmental reasons. Some people believe that eating meat is necessary, while others argue that plant-based diets are a better alternative. Do you agree or disagree?

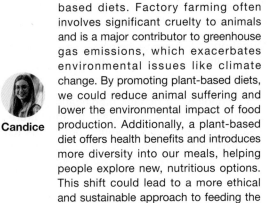

Candice

I would encourage a shift toward plant-based diets. Factory farming often involves significant cruelty to animals and is a major contributor to greenhouse gas emissions, which exacerbates environmental issues like climate change. By promoting plant-based diets, we could reduce animal suffering and lower the environmental impact of food production. Additionally, a plant-based diet offers health benefits and introduces more diversity into our meals, helping people explore new, nutritious options. This shift could lead to a more ethical and sustainable approach to feeding the global population.

Jake

While I understand Candice's viewpoint, I think a balanced approach is far more practical. A complete shift to plant-based diets may not be feasible for everyone due to factors like dietary needs, access to fresh produce, and cultural traditions. Instead of eliminating animal products entirely, I think we should focus on promoting more humane and sustainable farming practices. This approach would address concerns about animal welfare and environmental impact without forcing drastic dietary changes on those who may struggle to adopt a fully plant-based diet. Moderation and mindful consumption are key to making the food system more ethical and sustainable.

Copy | Cut | Paste | Word Count: 0 | Hide

PAGODA TOEFL

Actual Test

WRITING

PAGODA TOEFL

Actual Test

WRITING

PAGODA TOEFL

Actual Test

WRITING

3rd Edition

파고다교육그룹 언어교육연구소 | 저

PAGODA TOEFL

Actual Test Writing

해설서

PAGODA Books

3rd Edition

파고다교육그룹 언어교육연구소 | 저

PAGODA TOEFL

Actual Test Writing

해설서

PAGODA Books

Actual Test 01

본서 | p. 54

Question 1

Reading Passage

Due to their higher level of energy efficiency, many governments are advocating the use of compact fluorescent lamps (CFLs). While they may be superior to regular incandescent bulbs in many respects, research suggests that they are not the wonder solution that so many people seem to think they are.

높은 에너지 효율성 때문에 많은 정부는 콤팩트 형광등(CFLs)의 사용을 지지하고 있다. 많은 면에서 일반 백열등보다 우수할 수도 있지만, 연구는 콤팩트 형광등이 많은 사람이 생각하는 것처럼 놀라운 해결책은 아니라는 것을 보여준다.

Firstly, just like any other type of fluorescent lamp, CFLs contain mercury. They may last a long time, but eventually they must be replaced, and mercury is highly toxic. If they are put in landfills, the mercury could leak out into the water table and rivers, poisoning the fish and people. The mercury is also a hazard for people who work in recycling plants because the bulbs are easily broken.

첫째, 다른 모든 형태의 형광등처럼 콤팩트 형광등은 수은을 함유하고 있다. 오랜 기간 지속될 수 있지만 결국에는 교체되어야 하고, 수은은 독성이 매우 강하다. 만약 쓰레기 매립지에 버려진다면 수은이 지하수면과 강으로 스며 나와 어류와 사람들을 중독시킬 수 있다. 수은은 또한 재활용 공장에서 일하는 사람들에게 해가 되는데, 이것은 전구가 쉽게 깨지기 때문이다.

Secondly, CFLs are pretty expensive. Depending on the size and wattage, they can cost 3 to 10 times as much as the bulbs they are meant to replace. These prices are unlikely to go down for some time as the technology is still being refined. Unless the government intends to mandate lower prices for the lamps, it would put the financial burden on consumers, especially on companies in large buildings.

둘째, 콤팩트 형광등은 상당히 비싸다. 크기와 전력량에 따라 그것들은 교체하고자 하는 전구에 비해 3~10배의 비용이 든다. 기술이 여전히 개량 중이기 때문에 이 가격은 당분간 내려갈 것 같지 않다. 정부가 이 전등에 낮은 가격을 강제하지 않는 한 소비자들, 특히 큰 건물에 있는 회사들에 재정적인 부담을 주게 될 것이다.

Finally, although they produce light more efficiently, the quality of that light is lower. Brighter lamps are a good thing, but the chemicals these lights use produce a much narrower spectrum of visible light. This harsher light is likely to irritate people who are using them; just as conventional fluorescent bulbs often give people sore eyes and headaches.

마지막으로, 콤팩트 형광등은 빛을 더 효과적으로 발하지만, 빛의 질은 더 낮다. 더 밝은 전등은 좋은 것이긴 하지만 이러한 빛이 사용하는 화학 물질들은 더 좁은 범위의 가시광선을 생산한다. 이 강한 빛은 그것을 사용하는 사람들을 자극하기 쉽다. 이는 전통적인 형광등이 종종 사람들의 눈을 아프게 하고 두통을 일으키는 것과 마찬가지이다.

어휘

energy efficiency 에너지 효율(성) | **advocate** ⓥ 지지하다, 옹호하다 | **compact fluorescent lamp** 콤팩트 형광등 | **incandescent bulb** 백열등 | **mercury** ⓝ 수은 | **landfill** ⓝ 쓰레기 매립지 | **leak out** 새어 나오다 | **water table** ⓝ 지하수면 | **hazard** ⓝ 위험 | **wattage** ⓝ 전력량 | **mandate** ⓥ 명령하다, 지시하다 | **visible light** 가시광선 | **irritate** ⓥ 자극하다 | **conventional** ⓐⓓⓙ 전통적인, 종래의

Lecture Script

AT01

The author of this reading raised some valid concerns about compact fluorescent lights, but he seems to be using outdated information. When viewed objectively, CFLs are clearly the better product in every way, and they should be used to replace incandescent lamps as soon as possible.

이 지문의 저자는 콤팩트 형광등에 관해 몇 가지 타당한 우려를 표했지만, 오래된 정보를 사용하고 있는 것 같습니다. 객관적으로 봤을 때 콤팩트 형광등은 분명히 모든 면에서 더 나은 제품이고, 따라서 가능한 한 빨리 백열등을 대신해서 사용되어야 합니다.

The first point he raised is absolutely true. CFLs do contain mercury, about 3 to 5 milligrams per bulb; although, some newer eco-friendly versions have lowered that to about 1 milligram. However, the amount of mercury this would release into the environment is just a tiny fraction of what is pumped into the air by coal-fired power plants. With their increased efficiency, widespread use of CFLs would greatly reduce the overall amount of mercury that pollutes our air and water every year.

그가 제시한 첫 번째 의견은 전적으로 사실입니다. 비록 최신 친환경 제품은 수은을 1mg 정도까지 낮추기는 했지만 콤팩트 형광등은 전구 한 개에 약 3~5mg의 수은을 함유하고 있습니다. 그러나 이로 인해 환경으로 배출되는 수은의 양은 화력 발전소에서 대기로 배출하는 양에 비하면 매우 적은 일부입니다. 개선된 효율성과 함께 콤팩트 형광등의 광범위한 사용은 매년 대기와 수질을 오염시키는 수은의 총량을 매우 감소시킬 것입니다.

His second point about the high price is also true, but only on the surface of it. To produce the same light output as incandescent bulbs, CFLs use only 20 to 30 percent as much electricity. On top of that, they last from 8 to 15 times longer. So, if you do the math, they are actually much cheaper. Consumers would need to replace them far less often, and they would have lower electric bills as well. Not only that, but many are designed to fit into lamps manufactured for incandescent bulbs, so people can still use their old appliances.

높은 가격에 대한 저자의 두 번째 의견 역시 사실이지만, 그것은 겉으로 볼 때만 그렇습니다. 콤팩트 형광등은 백열등이 같은 빛을 내는 데 쓰는 전기의 약 20~30%만을 사용합니다. 게다가 8~15배 정도 더 오래 갑니다. 따라서 계산해 보면 콤팩트 형광등이 실제로 훨씬 더 저렴합니다. 소비자들은 전등을 교체하는 빈도수가 훨씬 줄어들 뿐 아니라 더 낮은 금액의 전기요금 청구서를 받게 될 것입니다. 그뿐 아니라 콤팩트 형광등은 백열등을 위해 만들어진 전등에 맞도록 제작되기 때문에 사람들은 원래 가지고 있던 기기들을 그대로 사용할 수 있습니다.

His third point was true when the bulbs were first being produced, but as he said, the technology is still advancing. The current blend of chemicals used in CFLs is far more pleasing to the eye. By increasing the variety of phosphorous bearing

저자의 세 번째 의견은 전구가 처음 생산되었을 때는 맞는 말이었지만, 그가 말했듯 이 기술은 여전히 발전하고 있습니다. 콤팩트 형광등에 사용되는 화학 물질의 현재 조합은 눈에 더욱 편안합니다. 인을 함유한 화합물을 훨씬 더 다양하게 만듦으로써 콤

compounds, they emit more of the visible spectrum, producing a warmer, less harsh light.

팩트 형광등은 더 많은 가시 스펙트럼을 발산하여 더 따뜻하고 덜 자극적인 빛을 생산합니다.

어휘

valid adj 타당한 | **outdated** adj 오래된 | **objectively** adv 객관적으로 | **eco-friendly** adj 친환경적인 | **fraction** n 일부, 부분 | **coal-fired power plant** 화력 발전소 | **appliance** n 기기 | **blend** n 혼합, 조합 | **pleasing** adj 기분 좋은, 만족스러운 | **phosphorous** adj 인을 함유한

Sample Summary

The reading and the lecture both talk about the positive and negative aspects of mandating the replacement of incandescent light bulbs with compact fluorescent bulbs. The reading proposes that this is a premature solution, but the lecture maintains that such a mandate is the best option.

지문과 강의 둘 다 백열등을 콤팩트 형광등으로 교체하는 것을 강제하는 것의 긍정적 측면과 부정적 측면에 관해 이야기하고 있다. 지문은 이것이 시기상조의 해결책이라고 주장하지만, 강의에서는 그러한 지시가 최선의 선택이라고 주장한다.

Firstly, the reading points out that CFLs are dangerous because they contain mercury just like any other fluorescent light bulb. The lecturer admits that this is true, but goes on to point out that widespread use of them would reduce the overall amount of mercury released into the environment. This is because their efficiency would reduce the amount of coal burned for power, thereby reducing emission of mercury into the atmosphere.

첫째, 지문은 콤팩트 형광등이 다른 형광등과 마찬가지로 수은을 함유하고 있으므로 위험하다고 지적한다. 강의자는 이것이 사실이라고 인정하지만, 콤팩트 형광등의 광범위한 사용이 환경으로 유출되는 전체 수은의 양을 줄일 것이라고 지적한다. 이는 콤팩트 형광등의 효율성이 전기를 생산하기 위해 연소되는 석탄의 양을 감소시키고, 따라서 대기로의 수은 배출물을 줄이기 때문이다.

Secondly, the reading contends that CFLs are too expensive and would place an unnecessary burden on consumers. Again, the lecturer concedes that they are expensive to purchase. However, he then explains that with their increased efficiency, longer life, and compatibility with incandescent light fixtures, they are actually far cheaper in the long term.

둘째, 지문은 콤팩트 형광등이 너무 비싸고 소비자들에게 불필요한 부담을 줄 것이라고 주장한다. 다시 한번 강의자는 그것이 구매하기에 비싸다는 것을 인정한다. 하지만 그는 효율 증대와 더 긴 수명, 백열등 조명 기구와의 호환성으로 콤팩트 형광등이 사실 장기적으로 훨씬 더 저렴하다고 설명한다.

Thirdly, the author complains that CFLs produce lower quality light than incandescent bulbs, which could cause health problems. The lecturer admits that this was initially true, but contends that the technology has advanced. The chemical mixture inside the bulbs has been improved and they now emit better quality light.

셋째, 저자는 콤팩트 형광등이 백열등보다 질이 더 낮은 빛을 내는데, 그것이 건강 문제를 야기할 수 있다고 불만을 표한다. 강의자는 이것이 초기에는 사실이었다는 것을 인정하지만 기술이 발전했다고 주장한다. 전구 안의 화학 혼합물이 개선되어 콤팩트 형광등은 현재 더 나은 질의 빛을 발산한다.

어휘

replacement n 교체 | **premature** adj 시기상조의 | **point out** 지적하다 | **widespread** adj 광범위한 | **thereby** adv 그렇게 함으로써 | **emission** n 배출 | **concede** v 인정하다 | **compatibility** n 호환성 | **light fixture** 조명 기구

Question 2

Academic Discussion Task

Your professor is teaching a class. Write a post responding to the professor's question.

당신의 교수님께서 강의 중입니다. 교수님의 질문에 답하는 글을 쓰세요.

In your response, you should:
- express and support your opinion
- make a contribution to the discussion

- 당신의 의견을 표현하고 뒷받침하세요
- 토론에 기여하세요

An effective response will contain at least 100 words.
You will have 10 minutes to write it.

효과적인 답변은 최소한 100단어를 포함할 것입니다.
당신은 10분 동안 글을 작성할 수 있습니다.

Dr. Robert: Some people believe that universities are justified in investing in sports activities, while others argue that education should be prioritized. Which position do you agree with?

로버트 교수: 일부 사람들은 대학이 스포츠 활동에 투자하는 것이 정당하다고 생각하지만, 다른 사람들은 교육이 우선시되어야 한다고 주장합니다. 당신은 어느 입장에 동의합니까?

Paul: I personally believe that sports programs should receive equal funding to education. Plato argued that both physical development and intellectual development are essential to success. Investing in sports only furthers the idea that a healthy mind should exist in balance with a healthy body. I also believe that sports teams are a great venue for students to take part in healthy competition, finding unity in their school colors, but also being driven to excel.

폴: 저는 개인적으로 스포츠 프로그램이 교육과 동일한 자금을 받아야 한다고 생각합니다. 플라톤은 신체적 발달과 지적 발달이 모두 성공에 필수적이라고 주장했습니다. 스포츠에 투자하는 것은 건강한 마음이 건강한 신체와 균형을 이루어야 한다는 생각을 더욱 발전시키는 것입니다. 저는 또한 스포츠팀은 학생들이 건전한 경쟁에 참여하고, 학교 색상 속에서 단결을 찾으면서도 뛰어난 성과를 내도록 동기를 부여하는 훌륭한 장이라고 생각합니다.

Rebecca: My opinion leans toward more emphasis on education. A university is a place of learning. If, as Paul is implying, it is a place for sports as well, then every university student should be on a sports team. Sports do not equate to physical education; I believe such education takes place in actual classes that teach sports and physical skills, and for which the student

레베카: 저는 교육에 더 중점을 두어야 한다고 생각합니다. 대학은 학문의 장소입니다. 만약 폴이 암시하는 것처럼 대학이 스포츠를 위한 장소이기도 하다면, 모든 대학생은 스포츠팀에 속해야 할 것입니다. 스포츠는 체육 교육과 동일하지 않습니다. 저는 그러한 교육이 스포츠와 신체적 기술을 가르치는 실제 수업에서 이루어지며, 그 수업에서 학생들이 학점을 받는다고 생각합니다. 따라서 제가 말하

receives credits. Thus, in line with the distinction I am trying to make, investing in facilities for better physical education classes would make more sense than funding competitive athletic programs that the vast majority of students cannot participate in, beyond being spectators.

고자 하는 차이점에 따라, 대다수의 학생이 관중으로만 참여할 수 있는 경쟁적인 운동 프로그램에 자금을 지원하는 것보다 더 나은 체육 수업을 위한 시설에 투자하는 것이 더 합리적일 것입니다.

어휘

prioritize v 우선시하다 | **personally** adv 개인적으로 | **physical** adj 신체적인, 육체적인 | **intellectual** adj 지적인 | **venue** n 장, 기회 | **take part in** 참여하다 | **competition** n 경쟁 | **unity** n 단결 | **be driven to** ~하도록 동기부여되다 | **excel** v 뛰어나다 | **emphasis** n 강조 | **imply** v 암시하다 | **equate** v 동일시하다 | **distinction** n 구별 | **competitive** adj 경쟁적인 | **athletic** adj 운동의

Sample Response

While I see where Paul is coming from, my opinion aligns more with Rebecca's. Team sports are not an important part of university life. As a matter of fact, I'd like to go a step further and argue that paying high tuition for physical education at a university doesn't make sense either. Universities should focus their funding on things that can only be learned at an institution of higher education, and not things we can learn to do at the park or local gymnasium. Diverting funding from sports teams and physical education to higher-quality laboratories, libraries, and technology in our classrooms would make more sense to me. Moreover, while we are on the topic of tuition, funding for sports should also be redirected towards academic scholarships and grants. Students who are drowning in student loan debt should be asking why schools are wasting money on things that don't enhance their education in any way.

폴의 입장을 이해하지만, 제 의견은 레베카의 의견에 더 가깝습니다. 팀 스포츠는 대학 생활의 중요한 부분이 아닙니다. 사실, 저는 한 걸음 더 나아가 대학에서 체육 교육에 높은 등록금을 지불하는 것도 말이 되지 않는다고 주장하고 싶습니다. 대학은 공원이나 지역 체육관에서 배울 수 있는 것이 아닌, 고등 교육 기관에서만 배울 수 있는 것들에 자금을 집중해야 한다고 생각합니다. 스포츠팀과 체육 교육에 할당된 자금을 더 높은 품질의 실험실, 도서관, 그리고 교실의 기술로 전환하는 것이 더 합리적이라고 봅니다. 또한, 등록금 문제를 논의하는 김에, 스포츠에 대한 자금도 학업 장학금과 보조금으로 전환되어야 합니다. 학자금 대출 부채에 허덕이는 학생들은 학교가 그들의 교육에 아무런 도움이 되지 않는 것에 왜 돈을 낭비하고 있는지 의문을 가져야 할 것입니다.

어휘

align v 정렬하다 | **local** adj 지역의 | **divert** v 전환하다 | **laboratory** n 실험실 | **redirect** v 방향을 바꾸다 | **grant** n 장학금 | **drown in** ~에 파묻히다, ~에 허덕이다 | **student loan debt** 학자금 대출 부채 | **enhance** v 향상시키다

Actual Test 02

본서 | p. 58

Question 1

Reading Passage

Of all the sharks that swim in the oceans, none has such a distinct profile as the hammerhead shark. The hammer-shaped elongated head for which it is named makes it instantly recognizable, and it has invited speculation for centuries. Obviously, such a radical alteration in shape must be an adaptation, but for what purpose?

바다에서 헤엄치는 모든 상어 중 귀상어처럼 특징적인 옆모습을 가진 상어는 없다. 이름이 말해주듯, 망치 모양의 길게 쭉 뻗은 머리는 즉시 그것을 알아보기 쉽게 해주며, 수 세기 동안 추측을 불러일으켰다. 그러한 생김새의 급격한 변화는 명백히 적응의 결과인데, 그렇다면 그 목적은 무엇일까?

Due to the shape of their heads and their relatively small mouths, some have proposed that the hammer-shaped head is used as a weapon. Hammerheads typically hunt near the sea floor, and they could use their head to strike prey, slamming it into the ground. Indeed, some hammerheads have been observed holding their prey down while they devour it. A more normally shaped head would make this tactic difficult if not impossible to carry out.

머리 모양과 상대적으로 작은 입 때문에 어떤 사람들은 망치 모양의 머리가 무기로 사용된다고 주장한다. 귀상어들은 전형적으로 해저 가까이에서 사냥을 하며, 머리를 사용하여 먹이를 쳐서 땅으로 처박는다. 실제로 어떤 귀상어들은 먹이를 먹는 동안 먹이를 거꾸로 잡은 모습이 관찰되기도 했다. 좀 더 평범한 모양의 머리였다면 불가능하진 않지만 이 전략을 시행하기 힘들었을 것이다.

The wide flat shape of the head may serve another physical purpose, which is acting as a kind of hydrofoil. Other species of shark are dedicated to moving in more or less a straight line once they begin a strike. However, hammerheads have been observed rapidly changing direction, and their head could be the reason. Much like the wings of an airplane, the head shape could provide lift in the water. This additional energy could easily be channeled into making sharper turns while pursuing prey.

넓고 납작한 모양의 머리는 또 다른 신체적인 기능을 하는데, 일종의 수중익선 역할을 하는 것이다. 다른 종들의 상어는 일단 가격을 시작하고 나면 직선으로 움직이는 데 전념한다. 하지만 귀상어는 급격하게 방향을 바꾸는 것이 목격되었으며, 이들의 머리가 그 이유일 수 있다. 비행기의 날개처럼 머리 모양은 물속에서 양력을 제공한다. 이러한 추가적인 에너지로 먹이를 쫓는 동안 더욱 재빠르게 방향을 틀 수 있게 된다.

The hammer shape may also serve the purpose of increasing their sensory ability. Like most species of shark, hammerheads have electro-sensory organs located on the underside of their snouts. These sensitive organs allow them to detect

망치 모양은 또한 감각 능력을 증가하는 목적에 알맞다. 대부분의 상어와 마찬가지로 귀상어는 주둥이 아래쪽에 위치한 전기 지각 기관을 가지고 있다. 이러한 민감한 기관은 모든 동물이 방출하는 흐릿한 전기 신호를 감지할 수 있게 하여 상어가 먹이를

the faint electrical signals that all animals emit, allowing the sharks to track their prey more easily. The increased number of sensory organs would compensate for the limited field of vision their eye placement would cause.

더욱 쉽게 추적할 수 있도록 해준다. 더 많아진 감각 기관은 눈 위치 때문에 야기되는 제한된 시야를 보완해줄 것이다.

어휘

profile n 옆모습 | **hammerhead shark** 귀상어 | **elongated** adj 가늘고 긴 | **speculation** n 추측 | **alteration** n 변화 | **adaptation** n 적응 | **slam** v 세게 던지다 | **devour** v 걸신 들린 듯 먹다 | **hydrofoil** n 수중익선 | **lift** n 양력 | **channel** v 돌리다, 쏟다 | **electro-sensory** adj 전기 지각의 | **snout** n 코, 주둥이 | **compensate for** 보상하다, 보완하다

Lecture Script

AT02

In yesterday's reading assignment, you were presented with three theories that have been suggested to explain the unique head shape for which hammerhead sharks are named. All of these theories have received a good deal of support over the years; however, they do not stand up to closer scrutiny.

어제 읽기 과제에서 여러분들은 귀상어에게 그 이름을 갖게 한 독특한 머리 모양을 설명하기 위해 제안된 세 가지 이론을 접했을 겁니다. 이 세 가지 이론은 모두 수년 동안 많은 지지를 받아온 것들이지만 그것들은 자세히 살펴보면 허점이 드러납니다.

Firstly, the author explains that the sharks may use their hammer-shaped heads as a weapon, and cites an example of just such behavior. However, the incidents he is referring to involve only one out of the nine total species of hammerheads: the great hammerhead. These sharks have a heavy, flat head which allows them to attack and pin their favorite prey, stingrays. However, the other eight species have smaller, often more angled heads that would be ill-suited to this technique. Therefore, this theory only applies to a further adaptation for one species, and does not explain the overall evolution of hammerheads.

첫째로, 저자는 상어가 망치 모양의 머리를 무기로 사용할지도 모른다고 설명하며 그러한 행동의 한 예를 들고 있습니다. 하지만 그가 언급한 사례들은 전체 아홉 종의 귀상어 중 오직 한 종, 그레이트 해머헤드에만 해당합니다. 이 상어는 무겁고 납작한 머리를 가지고 있으며 이는 그들이 가장 좋아하는 먹이인 가오리를 공격하여 꼼짝 못 하게 해줍니다. 하지만 다른 여덟 종의 상어들은 작고 종종 더 각진 머리를 가지고 있는데 이는 이러한 기술에 적합하지 않습니다. 그러므로 이 이론은 오직 한 종의 심화된 적응에만 적용될 뿐이며, 귀상어의 전반적인 진화를 설명하지는 않습니다.

Next, he discusses the possibility that their head shape may improve their maneuverability. While they definitely change direction more rapidly than other species, hammerheads do not owe this ability to their head shape. In fact, dissection has

다음으로, 저자는 귀상어의 머리 모양이 기동력을 향상해준다는 가능성에 대해 논하고 있습니다. 그들이 확실히 다른 종보다는 방향을 급속하게 바꿀 수 있기는 하지만, 귀상어의 이러한 능력은 그들의 머리 모양 때문에 비롯된 것이 아닙니다. 사실 해부

revealed that they owe their maneuverability to their neck structure. Hammerheads have a more flexible spine and unique musculature in their necks which allow them to bend their bodies and turn much faster.

를 해본 결과, 그들의 기동력은 목의 구조 때문에 나오는 것이었습니다. 귀상어는 목에 더욱 유연한 척추와 독특한 근육 조직을 가지고 있어 몸을 구부리고 훨씬 더 빠르게 방향을 틀 수 있게 해줍니다.

Finally, he mentions a theory that proposes that their head shape allows them to have better sensory perception. While it is true that they have more widely spaced electro-sensory organs, an even greater benefit comes from their eye placement. He says that having eyes located at the ends of the hammer limits the sharks' vision. However, experiments have disproven this utterly. In fact, the eyes give the shark full 360 degree vertical vision. Not only that, but the eyes are angled forward, which gives them an overlap of 48 degrees in their binocular vision, which is far superior to the 10 degrees observed in sharks with conventionally shaped heads.

마지막으로, 저자는 귀상어의 머리 모양이 더 좋은 감각 인지력을 갖도록 해주었다고 주장하는 이론을 언급합니다. 귀상어에게 전기 지각 기관이 더 넓게 분포되어 있다는 것은 사실이지만, 훨씬 더 큰 이점은 눈의 위치에서 옵니다. 저자는 귀상어의 눈이 망치 모양 머리의 끝에 있는 것이 상어의 시야를 제한한다고 했습니다. 하지만 실험에 의해 이것이 완전히 틀렸다는 것이 증명되었습니다. 실제로 그들의 눈은 상어에게 완벽한 360도 수직 시야를 제공합니다. 그뿐 아니라 눈이 앞쪽을 향하고 있어서 이로 인해 쌍안시에서 48도의 겹치는 부분이 생기는데, 이는 전통적인 모양의 머리를 가진 상어들에게서 관찰되는 10도보다 훨씬 더 우수합니다.

어휘

assignment n 과제 | **stand up to** ~에 맞서다, 저항하다 | **scrutiny** n 철저한 검토 | **pin** v 꼼짝 못하게 하다 | **ill-suited** adj 어울리지 않는 | **maneuverability** n 기동성 | **dissection** n 해부 | **musculature** n 근육 조직 | **utterly** adv 완전히 | **vertical** adj 수직의 | **angled** adj 각이 진, 치우친 | **binocular vision** 쌍안시 (두 눈으로 보는 시력)

Sample Summary

The reading passage provides three theories that have been commonly quoted to explain the reason for the hammerhead shark's unique head shape.

읽기 지문은 귀상어의 독특한 머리 모양에 대한 이유를 설명하는 데 흔히 인용되는 세 가지 이론을 제시한다.

The first theory suggests that the shark's head has evolved into such a shape to maximize its effectiveness as a bludgeoning weapon. The passage states that hammerhead sharks use their head to pin down their prey. However, the lecturer points out that only the great hammerhead shark—one out of nine species of hammerhead—uses its head to strike its prey in that manner.

첫 번째 이론은 상어의 머리가 때리는 무기로서의 효율성을 극대화하기 위해 그러한 모양으로 진화한 것이라고 주장한다. 지문에서는 귀상어가 머리를 사용하여 먹이를 꼼짝 못 하게 한다고 설명한다. 하지만 강의자는 아홉 종의 귀상어 중 오직 한 종인 그레이트 해머헤드만 이러한 방식으로 머리를 사용하여 먹이를 가격한다고 지적하고 있다. 그러므로 첫 번째 이론은 모든 귀상어 종에 해당하는 설명을

Therefore, the first theory doesn't provide an explanation that encompasses all hammerhead species.

제공하지 못한다.

The second theory mentioned in the reading passage states that the unique head shape allows hammerhead sharks to change directions faster. While the lecturer does concede that hammerhead sharks are known to change directions more fluidly and rapidly than other sharks, he contends that the factor that allows for this increased maneuverability is not the head shape. Rather, it is the hammerhead's neck structure. Hammerheads have a more flexible spine, which allows them to change directions faster.

읽기 지문에서 언급된 두 번째 이론은 독특한 머리 모양이 귀상어가 방향을 더 빠르게 전환하게 해준다고 설명한다. 강의자는 귀상어가 다른 상어들보다 더욱더 유동적이고 빠르게 방향을 전환하는 것으로 알려졌다는 것은 인정하지만, 이러한 향상된 기동력을 가능하게 하는 요소는 그들의 머리 모양이 아니라고 주장한다. 오히려 그것은 귀상어의 목 구조이다. 귀상어는 더 유연한 척추를 가지고 있어서 방향을 더 빠르게 전환할 수 있는 것이다.

Lastly, the author of the reading passage states that the unique head shape allows hammerheads to be extremely sensitive to electro-sensory signals. This heightened sensitivity allows hammerheads to track down prey more easily. This also compensates for hammerhead's limited field of vision due to their eye placement. However, the lecturer contradicts this by saying that the hammerhead's eye placement actually allows for full 360 degree vertical vision. This is definitely an advantage, not a limitation.

마지막으로, 읽기 지문의 저자는 독특한 머리 모양으로 인해 귀상어가 전기 지각 신호에 극도로 예민하다고 설명한다. 이 강화된 민감성은 귀상어가 먹이를 더욱 쉽게 찾아낼 수 있게 해준다. 이것은 또한 눈의 위치로 인해 발생하는 귀상어의 한정된 시야를 보완해 준다. 하지만 강의자는 귀상어의 눈의 위치가 사실상 완벽한 360도 수직 시야를 가능하게 해준다고 설명하며 이를 반박한다. 이것은 분명히 한계가 아니라 이점이다.

어휘

maximize v 극대화하다 | **bludgeon** v 때리다 | **encompass** v 포함하다 | **fluidly** adv 유연하게 | **heighten** v 강화하다, 고조되다 | **track down** ~을 찾아내다 | **contradict** v 반박하다

Question 2

Academic Discussion Task

Your professor is teaching a class. Write a post responding to the professor's question.

당신의 교수님께서 강의 중입니다. 교수님의 질문에 답하는 글을 쓰세요.

In your response, you should:
- express and support your opinion
- make a contribution to the discussion

- 당신의 의견을 표현하고 뒷받침하세요
- 토론에 기여하세요

An effective response will contain at least 100 words.
You will have 10 minutes to write it.

Dr. Jay: Nowadays, there is a lot of emphasis put on honesty. Our interpersonal communications textbook is no exception. It also stresses the need for communicators to speak truthfully and honestly. It argues that honesty builds trust, encourages cooperation, and strengthens bonds. But do you think this is always the case? Do you agree or disagree that there are situations in which telling a lie is better than telling the truth?

Paul: I believe it's best to hold fast to what our textbook teaches. Think about situations where we consider telling a small, seemingly harmless lie. Let's say you're a mother who was diagnosed with a serious illness. Many would consider lying to their children to protect them from the truth. Can you imagine how hurt the children would feel when they find out the truth? Instead of protecting them, you've hurt those closest to you. Instead, just as our textbook says, being honest is the right way. It can bring the family closer together, helping them cherish their time more and face the challenges ahead.

Rebecca: I agree with Paul. In my personal experience, I can't tell you how many times I've been able to fix a problem simply by telling the truth. This has been the case specifically in situations where I considered withholding the truth. I simply can't operate when there is a lie that I need to maintain. Whenever I withhold information from someone, nothing is ever the same. I become someone else, and I need to constantly work to continue as if the lie were true. In the end, I do a disservice to myself, to those around me, and to the potential for a great future.

효과적인 답변은 최소한 100단어를 포함할 것입니다.
당신은 10분 동안 글을 작성할 수 있습니다.

제이 교수: 요즘 정직함의 중요성이 많이 강조되고 있습니다. 우리 대인관계 소통 교재도 예외는 아닙니다. 교재도 소통자들이 진실하고 정직하게 말해야 할 필요성을 강조하고 있습니다. 교재는 정직함이 신뢰를 쌓고, 협력을 장려하며, 유대감을 강화한다고 주장합니다. 하지만 이것이 항상 맞는 경우일까요? 거짓말을 하는 것이 진실을 말하는 것보다 더 나은 상황이 있다는 것에 동의하십니까, 반대하십니까?

폴: 저는 교재가 가르치는 대로 따르는 것이 최선이라고 생각합니다. 우리가 작은, 겉보기에 무해한 거짓말을 생각하는 것을 고려하는 상황을 떠올려 보세요. 예를 들어, 당신이 심각한 질병을 진단받은 어머니라고 가정해 봅시다. 많은 사람들은 아이들을 진실로부터 보호하기 위해 거짓말을 할 생각을 할 것입니다. 아이들이 나중에 진실을 알게 되었을 때 얼마나 상처받을지 상상할 수 있습니까? 그들을 보호하기는커녕, 오히려 가장 가까운 사람들에게 상처를 주게 되는 것입니다. 대신 우리 교재에서 말하는 것처럼 정직한 것이 옳은 길입니다. 가족을 더 가까이 이어주고, 함께하는 시간을 더 소중히 여기며 앞으로의 도전을 함께 마주할 수 있게 해 줄 것입니다.

레베카: 저도 폴의 의견에 동의합니다. 제 개인적인 경험에서, 제가 문제를 단순히 진실을 말함으로써 해결한 경우가 얼마나 많았는지 셀 수도 없습니다. 특히 진실을 숨기려 했던 상황에서 더욱 그러했습니다. 저는 유지해야 할 거짓말이 있을 때 도저히 정상적으로 행동할 수 없습니다. 누군가에게 정보를 숨길 때마다, 모든 것이 이전과 같지 않습니다. 저는 다른 사람이 되며, 거짓말을 사실인 것처럼 계속 유지하기 위해 끊임없이 애써야 합니다. 결국, 저는 저 자신과 주변 사람들, 그리고 멋진 미래의 가능성에 해를 끼치게 됩니다.

어휘

emphasis n 강조 | **honesty** n 정직 | **interpersonal** adj 대인 간의 | **communication** n 의사소통 | **stress** v 강조하다 | **truthfully** adv 진실하게 | **argue** v 주장하다 | **trust** n 신뢰 | **encourage** v 격려하다 | **cooperation** n 협력 | **strengthen** v 강화하다 | **bond** n 유대감 | **believe** v 믿다 | **hold fast to** ~에 고수하다 | **situation** n 상황 | **seemingly** adv 겉보기에는 | **harmless** adj 무해한 | **diagnose** v 진단하다 | **illness** n 질병 | **protect** v 보호하다 | **imagine** v 상상하다 | **hurt** v 상처 주다 | **honest** adj 정직한 | **cherish** v 소중히 여기다 | **challenge** n 도전 | **personal** adj 개인적인 | **withhold** v 숨기다 | **operate** v 행동하다 | **maintain** v 유지하다 | **constantly** adv 끊임없이 | **disservice** n 해를 끼침 | **potential** n 가능성

Sample Response

I do understand the merits of honesty. But I want to play devil's advocate and present a situation where I truly feel telling a lie would be more beneficial. I believe that lying is okay whenever I am doing so with the other person's best interests in mind. Let's say I am dating someone who has been honest with me about her insecurities regarding her appearance. One night, we get ready together to go on a date, and she spends hours looking for the right dress to wear for our night out. She finally settles on one, puts it on, scrutinizes herself in front of the mirror, and then turns to me, asking how she looks. As her boyfriend who has constantly been begging her to believe me when I say that I appreciate her just as she is, I will tell her she looks great, no matter what–even if the dress is not particularly flattering. Are my words unethical, even though I am only lying to boost her self-confidence? I don't think so.

저는 정직함의 장점을 이해합니다. 하지만 반대 입장을 대변하자면, 거짓말이 더 유익하다고 느끼는 상황을 제시하고 싶습니다. 상대방의 최선의 이익을 염두에 두고 거짓말을 한다면 괜찮다고 생각합니다. 예를 들어, 제가 사귀고 있는 사람이 자신의 외모에 대한 불안감을 솔직하게 털어놓았다고 가정해 보겠습니다. 어느 날 밤, 우리는 데이트 갈 준비를 같이하는데, 그녀는 우리의 밤 외출을 위해 몇 시간을 들여 적합한 드레스를 고릅니다. 마침내 한 드레스를 선택하고 입은 후, 거울 앞에서 자신을 꼼꼼히 살펴보고 나서 저에게 돌아서서 그녀가 어떻게 보이냐고 묻습니다. 저는 그녀에게 있는 그대로의 모습을 사랑한다고 끊임없이 확신시키려 했던 남자친구로서, 그 드레스가 꼭 어울리지 않더라도 그녀에게 멋지다고 말할 것입니다. 제가 그녀의 자존감을 높이기 위해 거짓말을 한대도 그것이 비윤리적인 것일까요? 저는 그렇지 않다고 생각합니다.

어휘

merit n 장점 | **devil's advocate** 반대 입장을 대변하는 사람 | **situation** n 상황 | **beneficial** adj 유익한 | **insecurity** n 불안 | **appearance** n 외모 | **scrutinize** v 세심히 살피다 | **appreciate** v 진가를 알아보다 | **flattering** adj 돋보이게 하는 | **unethical** adj 비윤리적인 | **boost** v 증진시키다 | **self-confidence** n 자신감

Actual Test 03

본서 | p. 62

Question 1

Reading Passage

An increasing number of companies have either adopted or are in the midst of considering the positive effects of a four-day workweek. Proponents of this policy argue that this would lead to greater gains for both employees as well as companies.

점점 더 많은 기업이 4일 근무제가 주는 긍정적인 영향을 도입했거나 도입을 검토 중이다. 이 정책의 지지자들은 이 정책이 직원과 회사 모두에게 더 큰 이익을 가져올 것이라고 주장하고 있다.

First, a shorter workweek can significantly enhance an employee's work-life balance. Burnout is becoming too common a problem these days. Shorter workweeks would allow workers to allocate more time to personal pursuits, hobbies, and family responsibilities, leading to improved mental health and overall well-being. With more time for rest and relaxation, employees are likely to return to work rejuvenated, keeping them happy.

첫째, 짧은 근무 주는 직원의 일과 삶의 균형을 크게 향상시킬 수 있다. 요즘 번아웃은 너무 흔한 문제가 되고 있다. 짧은 근무 주는 근로자들이 개인적인 추구, 취미, 그리고 가정 책임에 더 많은 시간을 할애할 수 있게 하여 정신 건강과 전반적인 웰빙을 개선시킬 것이다. 더 많은 휴식과 여가 시간을 통해 직원들은 활력을 되찾아 일터로 돌아올 가능성이 높아져 행복을 유지할 수 있다.

In addition, research suggests that shorter workweeks can lead to increased productivity and efficiency. By compressing work into fewer days, employees are often more focused and motivated to complete tasks within a shorter timeframe. This can result in reduced procrastination, fewer distractions, and higher levels of concentration during work hours. Moreover, as mentioned, an extra day off leaves employees with the opportunity to recharge, further resulting in higher-quality output.

또한, 연구에 따르면 짧은 근무 주는 생산성과 효율성을 높일 수 있다. 근무를 더 적은 날로 압축하면 직원들은 더 짧은 시간 안에 업무를 완료하려는 집중력과 동기가 높아진다. 이는 미루는 습관을 줄이고, 방해 요소를 감소시키며, 근무 시간 동안 더 높은 집중력을 발휘하게 할 수 있다. 게다가 앞서 언급했듯이, 하루 더 쉬는 날이 있으면 직원들이 재충전할 기회를 얻게 되어 더 높은 품질의 결과를 낼 수 있다.

Finally, offering flexible work arrangements such as a four-day workweek can make companies more attractive to prospective employees and enhance employee retention. In a competitive job market, organizations that prioritize employee well-being and offer innovative work arrangements

마지막으로, 4일 근무제와 같은 유연한 근무 방식을 제공하는 것은 기업이 잠재적인 직원들에게 더 매력적으로 보이게 하고, 직원 유지율을 높일 수 있다. 경쟁이 치열한 취업 시장에서 직원의 웰빙을 우선시하고 혁신적인 근무 방식을 제공하는 조직은 인재를 유치할 가능성이 더 높다. 또한, 자신이 가

are more likely to attract top talent. Additionally, employees who feel valued and supported by their employers are less likely to seek employment elsewhere, reducing turnover costs and fostering a more stable workforce.

치 있게 여겨지고 고용주로부터 지원을 받는다고 느끼는 직원들은 다른 곳에서 일자리를 찾을 가능성이 적어져 이직 비용을 줄이고 더 안정적인 인력을 유지할 수 있다.

어휘

adopt v 도입하다 | **midst** n 한가운데 | **proponent** n 지지자 | **significantly** adv 상당히 | **enhance** v 향상시키다 | **allocate** v 할당하다 | **pursuit** n 추구 | **overall** adj 전반적인 | **rejuvenated** adj 활력을 되찾은 | **productivity** n 생산성 | **efficiency** n 효율 | **compress** v 압축하다 | **procrastination** n 해야 할 일을 미루기 | **distraction** n 집중을 방해하는 것 | **recharge** v 재충전하다 | **output** n 생산량 | **work arrangement** 근무 형태 | **prospective** adj 잠재적인 | **retention** n 유지, 보유 | **prioritize** v 우선시하다 | **innovative** adj 혁신적인 | **turnover** n 이직률 | **foster** v 조성하다

Lecture Script

AT03

Hi class. Let's get straight into the reading. Although it makes some valid points, my biggest point of disagreement is the argument that shorter workweeks are in employees' best interests. Let's dive deeper so you can see what I mean by this.

안녕하세요, 여러분. 바로 본문으로 들어가 봅시다. 이 글은 몇 가지 타당한 점을 제시하고 있지만, 제가 가장 동의하지 않는 부분은 짧은 근무 주가 직원들에게 최선의 이익이라고 주장하는 부분입니다. 제가 무슨 말을 하는지 알 수 있도록 좀 더 깊이 들어가 보겠습니다.

First, the article argued that four-day workweeks would increase work-life balance. Don't get me wrong: I'm all for work-life balance. But there are those who argue that work-life balance can come at a big cost in terms of career progression. As you probably know, in many industries, advancement opportunities and salary increases are often tied to working longer hours or taking on additional responsibilities. Employees working fewer days would definitely find themselves at a disadvantage compared to others in their industry. This could potentially lead to feelings of frustration and slow career progress. Ultimately, the decreased motivation and morale among employees could undo all that's been gained through a better work-life balance.

먼저, 이 글은 4일 근무제가 일과 삶의 균형을 증진시킬 것이라고 주장했습니다. 오해하지 마세요. 저도 일과 삶의 균형을 지지합니다. 하지만 일부는 일과 삶의 균형이 커리어 발전에 큰 비용을 초래할 수 있다고 주장합니다. 여러분도 아시다시피, 많은 산업에서 승진 기회와 급여 인상은 종종 더 긴 시간 동안 일하거나 추가적인 책임을 맡는 것과 연관되어 있습니다. 더 적은 날을 일하는 직원들은 분명 그들의 업계에서 다른 사람들과 비교했을 때 불리한 입장에 처하게 될 것입니다. 이는 잠재적으로 좌절감과 경력 발전이 지체되는 느낌을 초래할 수 있습니다. 결국, 직원들 사이에서 동기 부여와 사기가 저하되면, 더 나은 일과 삶의 균형을 통해 얻어진 모든 것이 무너질 수 있습니다.

Next is the article's point about increased productivity. While I will concede that some

다음은 생산성 증가에 대한 글의 주장입니다. 짧은 근무 주가 생산성을 높인다는 일부 연구 결과를 인

research shows increased productivity with a shorter workweek, it's important to recognize that productivity gains may not be universal across all industries and job roles. Certain tasks or projects may require consistent, full-time attention, and reducing work hours could lead to delays or decreased output. Just think about how many industries out there require round-the-clock attention. Every change of shift involves an interruption and some reduction in productivity. My point is that companies really do need to think twice before they assume that this is the best way to improve their employees' performance.

정하지만, 생산성 향상이 모든 산업과 직무에서 보편적으로 적용되지는 않을 수 있다는 점을 인식하는 것이 중요합니다. 특정 업무나 프로젝트는 꾸준한 풀타임의 주의가 필요할 수 있으며, 근무 시간이 줄어들면 지연이나 생산성 저하로 이어질 수 있습니다. 24시간 주의가 필요한 많은 산업을 생각해 보세요. 교대가 바뀔 때마다 중단이 발생하고 생산성 감소가 따릅니다. 제 요점은, 기업들이 이것이 직원들의 성과를 향상시키는 최선의 방법이라고 단정 짓기 전에 두 번 생각해 봐야 한다는 것입니다.

Last, I want to talk about the argument that a four-day workweek would help companies attract better talent. Honestly, I think that's nonsense. We need to consider what a prospective employee takes into account when choosing a place to work. Surveys have consistently shown, for example, that people would rather work longer hours if they can get higher pay for doing so. People also look at insurance coverage, company perks, and company culture. It's important to take a more holistic approach to improving working conditions.

마지막으로, 4일 근무제가 더 나은 인재를 유치하는 데 도움이 된다는 주장에 대해 이야기하고 싶습니다. 솔직히, 저는 그 주장이 터무니없다고 생각합니다. 우리는 잠재적인 직원들이 직장을 선택할 때 무엇을 고려하는지 생각해 보아야 합니다. 예를 들어, 설문 조사는 사람들은 더 높은 보수를 받을 수 있다면 더 긴 시간을 일하는 것을 선호하는 경향이 있다고 꾸준히 나타내고 있습니다. 사람들은 또한 보험 혜택, 회사의 복지, 그리고 회사 문화를 고려합니다. 근무 조건을 개선하는 데 있어서는 보다 전체적인 접근이 중요하다고 생각합니다.

어휘

valid adj 유효한 | **progression** n 진행 | **advancement** n 발전 | **frustration** n 좌절감 | **career progress** 경력 발전 | **morale** n 사기, 의욕 | **productivity** n 생산성 | **concede** v 인정하다 | **consistent** adj 일관된 | **round-the-clock** adj 24시간 내내 | **attention** n 관심, 보살핌 | **shift** n 근무 교대조 | **performance** n 성과 | **take into account** 고려하다 | **insurance coverage** 보험 보장 범위 | **perk** n 특혜 | **holistic** adj 전체적인 | **working conditions** 근무 환경

Sample Summary

The potential effects of a four-day workweek are discussed in both the reading and the listening passage. While the reading insists on the merits of a shorter workweek, the lecture finds flaws in the passage's arguments.

4일 근무제가 미칠 수 있는 잠재적인 영향에 대해 본문과 강의에서 논의되고 있다. 본문은 짧은 근무주의 장점을 강조하는 반면, 강의는 본문의 주장에 결점이 있다고 지적하고 있다.

To begin with, while the text posits that a four-day workweek is an effective way to improve work-life balance, the lecturer points out that gaining a better work-life balance can also jeopardize long-term career goals. Shorter workweeks would lead to lower pay, fewer raises, and also fewer promotions. She ultimately questions the merits of improving work-life balance if it comes at the risk of impairing long-term growth, which is arguably more important.

우선, 본문에서는 4일 근무제가 일과 삶의 균형을 개선하는 효과적인 방법이라고 주장하고 있지만, 그녀는 더 나은 일과 삶의 균형을 얻는 것이 장기적인 커리어 목표를 위태롭게 할 수 있다고 지적하고 있다. 짧은 근무 주는 더 낮은 급여, 더 적은 임금 인상, 그리고 더 적은 승진 기회를 초래할 수 있다. 그녀는 더 중요할 수 있다는 주장도 있는 장기적인 성장을 저해할 위험이 있다면, 일과 삶의 균형을 개선하는 것이 과연 가치 있는지 의문을 제기하고 있다.

Moreover, the author believes that a four-day workweek would result in an increase in productivity through more compact work hours. However, the professor emphasizes that this is another opportunity to recognize that such workweeks would fail as a blanket policy. Though productivity would increase in some cases, it would decrease in cases where continuity is essential. Many industries require 24/7 operation, and interruptions due to short working hours would hurt productivity.

게다가, 저자는 4일 근무제가 더 압축된 근무 시간을 통해 생산성을 증가시킬 것이라고 믿고 있다. 그러나 교수는 그러한 근무 시간이 보편적인 정책으로는 실패할 것이라는 점을 인식해야 할 또 다른 기회라고 강조하고 있다. 일부 경우에는 생산성이 증가할 수 있지만, 연속성이 중요한 경우에는 생산성이 감소할 것이라는 것이다. 많은 산업은 연중무휴 운영이 필요하며, 짧은 근무 시간으로 인한 중단은 생산성에 해를 끼칠 것이다.

Finally, the professor challenges the idea that a four-day workweek would be enough to attract more talent to a company. She believes there are other more important factors when talented workers seek out companies, i.e., salary, benefits, and office environment. This directly rebuts the article's argument that four-day workweeks would be a major factor in attracting the most highly qualified applicants.

마지막으로, 교수는 4일 근무제가 더 많은 인재를 회사로 유치하기에 충분하다는 의견에 이의를 제기하고 있다. 그녀는 유능한 직원들이 회사를 선택할 때 더 중요한 요인들이 있다고 믿고 있으며, 그 예로 급여, 복지 혜택, 그리고 근무 환경을 들고 있다. 이는 4일 근무제가 가장 뛰어난 지원자들을 유치하는 주요 요인이 될 것이라는 본문의 주장에 직접적으로 반박하는 내용이다.

어휘

potential adj 잠재적인 | **merit** n 장점 | **flaw** n 결점, 결함 | **posit** v 단정하다 | **jeopardize** v 위험에 빠뜨리다 | **promotion** n 승진 | **impair** v 손상시키다 | **productivity** n 생산성 | **blanket** adj 포괄적인 | **essential** adj 필수적인 | **interruption** n 방해, 중단 | **rebut** v 반박하다 | **applicant** n 지원자

Question 2

Academic Discussion Task

Your professor is teaching a class. Write a post responding to the professor's question.

In your response, you should:
• express and support your opinion
• make a contribution to the discussion

An effective response will contain at least 100 words.
You will have 10 minutes to write it.

Dr. Bobby: Some people believe that maintaining strong relationships with existing friends and colleagues is more beneficial than meeting new people. Do you agree or disagree?

Ben: In my case, I happen to see more merit in expanding my network. I hate to say it, but we live in a world where we must recognize that we capitalize on everything, even our relationships. What can they bring to the table? How can I get back what I invest in someone else? What benefits does this person bring to my life? I don't think this can be helped, nor do I think it's morally wrong. The more we expand our network, the more we are able to expect returns. More connections mean more people to turn to when we need something. You simply have a greater chance of success the more relationships you forge.

Suzan: I happen to agree with Ben, that capitalizing on relationships is completely natural in today's world. However, I also believe that capitalizing on relationships works better if your relationships are of better quality. Say you operate like Ben, and you know hundreds of people at a shallow level. If one of them is a professor who, for example, could write a recommendation letter for your first-choice graduate school program, and you want to capitalize on that relationship, it's

당신의 교수님께서 강의 중입니다. 교수님의 질문에 답하는 글을 쓰세요.

• 당신의 의견을 표현하고 뒷받침하세요
• 토론에 기여하세요

효과적인 답변은 최소한 100단어를 포함할 것입니다.
당신은 10분 동안 글을 작성할 수 있습니다.

바비 교수: 어떤 사람들은 기존 친구 및 동료와의 관계를 유지하는 것이 새로운 사람을 만나는 것보다 더 유익하다고 생각합니다. 이에 동의하십니까, 반대하십니까?

벤: 제 경우에는 네트워크를 확장하는 데 더 큰 가치를 두고 있습니다. 이런 말을 하기 싫지만, 우리는 모든 것을, 심지어는 관계조차도 자본화해야 하는 세상에 살고 있음을 인정해야 합니다. 이 사람은 무엇을 제공할 수 있을까? 내가 다른 사람에게 투자한 것을 어떻게 되돌려 받을 수 있을까? 이 사람이 내 삶에 어떤 이점을 줄까? 저는 이것이 어쩔 수 없는 일이라고 생각하며, 도덕적으로도 잘못되었다고 생각하지 않습니다. 네트워크가 확장될수록 얻을 수 있는 보상도 커집니다. 더 많은 인맥이 있다는 것은 우리가 무언가 필요할 때 의지할 수 있는 사람이 더 많아진다는 의미입니다. 더 많은 관계를 맺을수록 성공할 확률이 높아집니다.

수잔: 저도 벤처럼 관계를 활용하는 것이 오늘날의 세상에서 자연스러운 일이라고 생각합니다. 하지만 저는 관계를 활용하는 것이 더 나은 관계일수록 더 효과적이라고 믿습니다. 벤처럼 수백 명의 사람들을 얕은 수준에서 알고 있다고 가정해 보겠습니다. 예를 들어, 그들 중 한 명이 내가 가장 선호하는 대학원 프로그램의 추천서를 써 줄 수 있는 교수인 경우라고 해도, 가끔 인사하는 정도로는 그 관계를 자본화해 합격 가능성에 영향을 주기 어려울 것입니다. 그것보다 더 깊은 관계가 필요합니다. 이것이

going to take more than just a few cursory greetings here and there to have an effect on your chances of getting into the program. It's going to take a deeper relationship than that. This is why I think everyone should focus on quality rather than quantity when it comes to human relationships.

제가 인간관계에서 양보다 질에 집중해야 한다고 생각하는 이유입니다.

어휘

maintain v 유지하다 | **existing** adj 기존의 | **beneficial** adj 유익한 | **merit** n 장점 | **expand** v 확장하다 | **capitalize on** ~을 활용하다 | **relationship** n 관계 | **invest** v 투자하다 | **benefit** n 이점 | **morally** adv 도덕적으로 | **expect** v 기대하다 | **return** n 수익 | **forge** v 구축하다 | **natural** adj 자연스러운 | **quality** n 질 | **operate** v 운영하다 | **shallow** adj 얕은 | **cursory** adj 피상적인 | **greeting** n 인사 | **effect** n 효과 | **chance** n 가능성 | **quantity** n 양 | **human relationship** 인간관계

Sample Answer

While I understand both Ben's and Suzan's respective perspectives on relationships, I strive to create genuine human relationships. And for me, that is only possible when I focus on the important people already in my life. These are the family members, the best friends, the teachers and mentors who have transformed my life. These are the connections that will last a lifetime. They are also the connections that enhance the time I spend in this lifetime. Ultimately, how could I possibly be comfortable with prioritizing new relationships over the people who have raised me and molded me into who I am? I surely hope they do the same for me. This is not to say that I don't enjoy making new friends. But assuming that the people already in my life are worth my time, I want to make sure I focus on them.

저는 벤과 수잔의 관계에 대한 각각의 관점을 이해하지만, 저는 진정한 인간관계를 형성하기 위해 노력합니다. 그리고 저에게 그것은 이미 제 삶에 있는 중요한 사람들에게 집중할 때만 가능합니다. 이들은 저의 삶을 변화시킨 가족, 가장 친한 친구, 선생님과 멘토들입니다. 이들이야말로 평생 지속될 관계들입니다. 그들은 또한 저에게 살아가는 동안의 시간을 더 의미 있게 만들어 주는 관계들입니다. 궁극적으로, 저를 성장시키고 지금의 저를 만들어 준 사람들보다 새로운 관계를 우선시하는 것이 어떻게 편할 수 있을까요? 저는 그들도 저에게 똑같이 해 주길 바랍니다. 새로운 친구를 사귀는 것을 즐기지 않는다는 뜻은 아닙니다. 하지만 이미 내 인생에 있는 사람들이 내 시간을 할애할 가치가 있다고 가정하면, 그들에게 집중하고 싶습니다.

어휘

respective adj 각각의 | **perspective** n 관점 | **genuine** adj 진정한 | **strive** v 노력하다 | **transform** v 변화시키다 | **enhance** v 향상시키다 | **ultimately** adv 궁극적으로 | **comfortable** adj (마음이) 편안한 | **prioritize** v 우선시하다 | **mold** v 형성하다 | **surely** adv 분명히 | **assume** v 가정하다 | **worth** adj ~의 가치가 있는

Actual Test 04

본서 | P. 66

Question 1

Reading Passage

In areas that often suffer from drought or severe storms, people sometimes use cloud seeding in order to increase or alter the precipitation they receive. Typically, silver iodide or dry ice is dropped into clouds, lowering their internal temperatures. The usefulness of this practice has been proven in many areas.

가뭄이나 거센 폭풍으로 고통받는 지역들에서 사람들은 강수량을 늘리거나 바꾸기 위해 때때로 '구름 씨 뿌리기'를 이용한다. 일반적으로 아이오딘화은이나 드라이아이스를 구름에 뿌려 구름 내부의 온도를 낮추는 것이다. 이렇게 하는 것의 유용함은 많은 분야에서 증명되었다.

In laboratory experiments, scientists created ideal conditions for hail formation and dispersed silver iodide into the clouds. The resultant precipitation was comparatively harmless snow as opposed to hailstones. This means that cloud seeding can be used both to limit the extent of damaging weather like hail as well as to promote snow or rainfall for beneficial reasons. In addition, this proves that the principle behind the idea of cloud seeding is sound.

실험실 실험에서 과학자들은 우박 형성에 이상적인 조건을 조성했고, 아이오딘화은을 구름에 뿌렸다. 그 결과로 생겨난 것은 우박이 아니라 비교적 위험하지 않은 눈이었다. 이는 구름 씨 뿌리기가 우박과 같은 기상 재해의 피해를 제한하는 것뿐 아니라 유익한 이유로 눈이나 비가 내리도록 촉진하는 데 사용될 수 있음을 의미한다. 또한 이는 구름 씨 뿌리기의 원리가 믿을 만한 것임을 증명한다.

North American scientists have proven the effectiveness of cloud seeding in the real world as well. One of the main threats to crops in the American Midwest is hail damage. Scientists flew airplanes into clouds that had the potential for creating hail and released chemicals. As a result, the clouds only dropped rain. Not only that, but the US government experimented with using silver iodide to weaken hurricanes. After releasing canisters of silver iodide into the eye wall of a hurricane, they observed a 10% drop in wind speeds.

북미의 과학자들은 실제 세계에서도 구름 씨 뿌리기의 효율성을 증명했다. 미국 중서부 농작물에게 가장 큰 위협 중 하나는 우박으로 인한 피해이다. 과학자들은 우박을 내리게 할 가능성이 있는 구름에 비행기를 보내어 화학물질들을 방출했다. 그 결과 그 구름은 비만 내리게 했다. 그뿐 아니라, 미국 정부는 허리케인을 약화시키기 위해 아이오딘화은을 이용하여 실험하기도 했다. 아이오딘화은이 든 통을 허리케인의 눈 벽에 날려 보낸 후, 그들은 풍속이 10% 감소한 것을 관찰했다.

Outside confirmation of the practical uses of cloud seeding has come from many other countries, including China. The Chinese regularly use the same techniques to prevent hail over cities as well

중국을 포함한 다른 많은 나라에서도 구름 씨 뿌리기의 활용이 확인되었다. 중국인들은 농장뿐만 아니라 도시에 우박이 내리는 것을 방지하기 위해 같은 기술을 정기적으로 이용한다. 그리고 강수량이

as farms. In addition, they have even used cloud seeding to cause beneficial precipitation when there was none to be had. In 1997, they were suffering from a prolonged drought, so scientists seeded clouds and created a heavy snowfall.

없으면 이로운 강수를 위해 구름 씨 뿌리기 기술을 사용해 왔다. 1997년 중국은 장기적인 가뭄으로 고생하고 있었기에 과학자들은 구름 씨 뿌리기를 이용하여 많은 양의 눈을 만들어 냈다.

어휘

alter v 바꾸다 | **precipitation** n 강수(량) | **silver iodide** 아이오딘화은 | **hail** n 우박 | **disperse** v 분산되다, 확산시키다 | **resultant** adj 그 결과로 생긴 | **canister** n 통 | **eye wall** 눈 벽 | **prolonged** adj 장기적인

Lecture Script

AT04

As you remember from the reading, many scientists claim to have used cloud seeding to create positive results. Don't misunderstand—I'm not saying that cloud seeding does not have great potential—however, the results those scientists have claimed are questionable at best.

Yes, in laboratory conditions, scientists have created clouds similar to those that commonly form hail. And yes, after seeding them with silver iodide, they did observe snowfall as opposed to hailstones. However, there is a very important phrase there: in laboratory conditions. It is much easier to achieve results in a controlled environment like a laboratory than it is in the real world. Weather is a chaotic system, and while intriguing, lab results are not a good indicator of effectiveness in the real world.

The results of the outdoor experiments carried out in the United States are also rather suspect. Firstly, the farmland that cloud seeding was carried out did experience fewer hailstorms than they would in an average season, but so did the surrounding areas. As for the hurricane tests... scientists have since learned that such fluctuations in wind strength are extremely common in hurricanes as their surroundings change. Therefore, both examples would appear

여러분이 읽기 자료에서 본 것을 기억하듯이 많은 과학자는 긍정적인 결과를 이끌어내기 위해 구름 씨 뿌리기를 이용했다고 주장합니다. 오해하지는 마세요. 구름 씨 뿌리기가 굉장한 가능성을 갖고 있지 않다고 말하려는 것은 아닙니다. 하지만 그 과학자들이 주장한 결과들은 아무리 낙관적으로 봐도 의심스럽습니다.

맞아요, 실험실의 조건에서 과학자들은 흔히 우박을 형성하는 것과 유사한 구름을 만들어 냈습니다. 그리고 아이오딘화은을 그 구름에 뿌린 뒤 우박 대신 눈이 오는 걸 관찰했다는 것도 맞습니다. 그러나 여기엔 매우 중요한 구절이 있습니다. "실험실의 조건에서"입니다. 실제 세계에서보다 실험실과 같은 통제된 환경에서 결과를 얻기가 훨씬 더 쉽습니다. 날씨는 혼란스러운 체계이고, 실험실에서의 결과는 흥미롭긴 해도 실제 세계에서의 효율성을 보여주는 좋은 지표가 아닙니다.

미국에서 행해진 야외 실험의 결과들 또한 의심스럽습니다. 먼저, 구름 씨 뿌리기를 했던 농지에 평년보다 우박이 덜 내린 것은 사실이지만, 근처 지역들 역시 마찬가지였어요. 허리케인 실험은... 과학자들은 후에 허리케인의 주변 환경이 바뀜에 따라 바람의 세기에 변동이 생기는 것은 극히 흔한 일이라는 것을 알게 되었습니다. 그러므로 두 가지 예 모두 인간의 개입으로 생겨났다기보다는 자연 현상 때문에 일어난 것처럼 보입니다.

to be more the product of natural phenomena than human intervention.

아시아에서의 실험은 언뜻 보기에는 완전히 성공한 것처럼 보이지만 현지 조건을 더 자세히 관찰하면 아닙니다. 그 실험은 대기 오염이 매우 심각한 지역인 베이징 근처에서 행해졌습니다. 오염된 공기 중에 주입된 미립자들은 종종 수증기를 끌어들이는데, 이는 구름을 더 차갑게 만들어 실제로 눈이 오게 만들 수 있습니다. 그러나 농가 지역은 공해가 적거나 아예 없는 경우가 대부분이기에 이곳에서의 실험은 잘 될 가능성이 작습니다. 그뿐 아니라 오염된 강수가 내리게 될 것이고, 이는 농업용으로나 사람이 사용하는 용으로나 적합하지 않습니다.

The experiment in Asia seems to be a complete success at first glance, but that is only until you examine the local conditions more closely. The test was carried out near Beijing, an area with extremely high air pollution. The particulates pumped into the air in pollution often attract water vapor, so making the clouds colder could indeed cause snow. However, most farming areas have little if any air pollution, so it would be less likely to work. Not only that, but the precipitation would be filled with pollution, which is ideal neither for farming nor human consumption.

어휘

questionable adj 의심스러운 | **at best** 잘해야, 아무리 낙관해도 | **intriguing** adj 매우 흥미로운 | **fluctuation** n 변동 | **intervention** n 조정, 간섭 | **particulates** n 미립자

Sample Summary

The reading passage mentions three different cases of how cloud seeding was used successfully to induce or alter precipitation. On the other hand, the lecturer casts doubt on the results reported by the reading passage.

읽기 지문은 강수를 유도하거나 바꾸기 위해 구름 씨 뿌리기가 어떻게 성공적으로 이용되었는지 세 가지 다른 사례들을 언급한다. 반면에 강의자는 읽기 지문에서 제시된 결과에 의문을 제기하고 있다.

The first case in the reading passage shows how cloud seeding caused precipitation to fall in the form of snow, which is harmless compared to hail. However, the lecturer points out that this result was produced in a laboratory setting, and therefore could not be said to be a true indicator of the effectiveness of cloud seeding.

읽기 지문의 첫 번째 사례는 구름 씨 뿌리기가 어떻게 강수가 우박과 비교해 위험하지 않은 눈의 형태로 내릴 수 있도록 했는지를 보여준다. 그러나 강의자는 이 결과가 실험실 환경에서 생성된 결과여서 구름 씨 뿌리기의 효율성을 입증하는 정확한 지표가 될 수는 없다고 지적한다.

In the second case, scientists in North America were able to produce a similar result in the real world. Silver iodide released into clouds resulted in rainfall instead of hail, and hurricane wind speeds were also decreased by 10%. Yet again,

두 번째 사례에서, 북미의 과학자들은 실제 세계에서 비슷한 결과를 얻을 수 있었다. 아이오딘화은을 구름에 뿌리자 우박 대신 비가 내렸고, 허리케인의 풍속 역시 10% 감소했다. 그러나 강의자는 이 성공적인 결과들이 인간의 활동보다는 자연환경에 더

the lecturer casts doubt on the author's claim by suggesting that these successful results were more influenced by natural conditions than human activity.

영향을 받은 것임을 제시하면서 저자의 주장에 의구심을 제기한다.

Lastly, the reading passage states that cloud seeding is also successfully practiced in China. Chinese scientists were able to utilize cloud seeding to prevent hail from falling and to create heavy snowfall in a prolonged drought. However, the lecturer contradicts this by explaining that the heavily polluted atmosphere was the main reason for heavy precipitation over that region. To make matters worse, the precipitation would contain pollutants, which wouldn't be beneficial to the crops and humans at all.

마지막으로 읽기 지문에서는 구름 씨 뿌리기가 중국에서 성공적으로 행해지고 있다고 진술한다. 중국의 과학자들은 우박이 내리는 것을 방지하고 지속되는 가뭄 시기에 많은 양의 눈이 내리게 하려고 구름 씨 뿌리기를 이용할 수 있었다. 그러나 강의자는 심각하게 오염된 대기가 그 지역에 큰 강수가 있었던 주원인이었다고 설명하면서 이를 반박한다. 설상가상으로 그 강수는 농작물과 사람에게 전혀 이롭지 않은 오염 물질을 포함하고 있을 것이다.

어휘

induce ⓥ 유도하다 | **indicator** ⓝ 지표 | **to make matters worse** 설상가상으로 | **pollutant** ⓝ 오염 물질

Question 2

Academic Discussion Task

Your professor is teaching a class. Write a post responding to the professor's question.

당신의 교수님께서 강의 중입니다. 교수님의 질문에 답하는 글을 쓰세요.

In your response, you should:
- express and support your opinion
- make a contribution to the discussion

- 당신의 의견을 표현하고 뒷받침하세요
- 토론에 기여하세요

An effective response will contain at least 100 words.
You will have 10 minutes to write it.

효과적인 답변은 최소한 100단어를 포함할 것입니다.
당신은 10분 동안 글을 작성할 수 있습니다.

Dr. Albert: Next week, we'll be discussing the various ways AI development could shape society, both positively and negatively. Before we dive into that in class, I'd like to get your input on this. I have an inquiry for the message board: "Should AI be heavily regulated, or should there be minimal restrictions?"

알버트 교수: 다음 주에는 인공지능의 발전이 사회를 긍정적으로 또는 부정적으로 변화시킬 수 있는 다양한 방식에 대해 논의할 예정입니다. 수업에 들어가기 전에 이에 대한 여러분의 의견을 듣고 싶습니다. 그래서 게시판에 질문이 하나 있습니다: "AI를 강력하게 규제해야 할까요, 아니면 최소한의 제한만 두어야 할까요?"

Jane: We need very strong regulations on artificial intelligence to mitigate potential risks. While AI can help solve complex problems, the possible harms it could cause, such as job displacement due to automation, are too significant to overlook. There are also ethical concerns, such as the misuse of data and violations of privacy, that need to be addressed. Without proper oversight, AI could create more harm than good. Therefore, I believe regulating AI will ensure that its development remains ethical and responsible, preventing societal disruption while still allowing for innovation in a controlled and thoughtful manner.

제인: 인공지능의 잠재적 위험을 완화하기 위해 매우 강력한 규제가 필요합니다. AI가 복잡한 문제를 해결하는 데 도움이 될 수 있지만, 자동화로 인한 일자리 상실과 같은 잠재적 피해는 간과하기에 너무 큽니다. 또한 데이터 오용과 사생활 침해와 같은 윤리적 문제들도 해결될 필요가 있습니다. 적절한 감독 없이는 AI가 이익보다 더 큰 해를 끼칠 수 있습니다. 따라서 저는 AI 규제가 그 개발이 윤리적이고 책임감 있게 진행되도록 보장하고, 사회적 혼란을 방지하는 동시에 통제되고 신중한 방식으로 혁신을 지속할 수 있게 해줄 것이라고 생각합니다.

Mark: I think overregulating artificial intelligence could stifle its potential for groundbreaking advancements. Therefore, minimal regulation would benefit society the most. While there are risks, such as job displacement and ethical concerns as Jane mentioned, AI also has immense potential to address critical challenges in fields like medicine, climate change, and space exploration. Instead of restricting its development, we should focus on ensuring responsible use of AI through guidelines and best practices. The true value of AI lies in how it is applied, and with the right approach, it can become a powerful tool for solving problems that humanity cannot tackle alone.

마크: 저는 인공지능을 과도하게 규제하는 것은 혁신적인 발전의 잠재력을 억제할 수 있다고 생각합니다. 따라서 최소한의 규제가 사회에 가장 큰 도움이 될 것입니다. 제인이 언급한 것처럼 일자리 상실이나 윤리적 문제 등의 위험이 있지만, AI는 또한 의학, 기후 변화, 우주 탐사와 같은 분야에서 중요한 문제를 해결할 수 있는 엄청난 잠재력을 가지고 있습니다. AI 개발을 제한하기보다는 지침과 모범 사례를 통해 AI의 책임 있는 사용을 보장하는 데 집중해야 합니다. AI의 진정한 가치는 그것이 어떻게 적용되는지에 있으며, 올바른 접근 방식을 취하면 그것은 인간이 혼자 해결할 수 없는 문제들을 해결하는 강력한 도구가 될 수 있습니다.

어휘

development n 개발 | **society** n 사회 | **minimal** adj 최소한의 | **regulation** n 규제 | **artificial intelligence** 인공지능 | **mitigate** v 완화하다 | **job displacement** 실직 | **automation** n 자동화 | **ethical** adj 윤리적인 | **misuse** n 오용 | **violation** n 위반 | **privacy** n 사생활 | **oversight** n 감독 | **responsible** adj 책임 있는 | **disruption** n 혼란 | **innovation** n 혁신 | **thoughtful** n 사려 깊은 | **manner** n 방식, 태도 | **overregulate** v 과잉 규제하다 | **stifle** v 억제하다 | **potential** n 잠재력 | **groundbreaking** adj 획기적인 | **advancement** n 발전 | **immense** adj 거대한 | **critical** adj 중요한 | **challenge** n 과제 | **climate change** 기후변화 | **guideline** n 지침 | **best practice** 모범 사례 | **approach** n 접근법 | **tackle** v 해결하다

Sample Response

Building on Jane's point, I think there's a growing issue of AI misuse in copying the likeness of celebrities and public figures that could be improved by strict regulations. With advancements in AI, especially in generating hyper-realistic images and deepfakes, celebrities are at risk of having their image used without consent, potentially damaging their reputation. Unscrupulous users can create AI-generated content that distorts their identity, leading to privacy violations and defamation. Therefore, regulations must be put in place to protect individuals from these harmful practices, ensuring that AI is not used to exploit or manipulate people's public image. This would uphold ethical standards while balancing innovation with accountability.

제인의 의견을 바탕으로, 저는 엄격한 규제를 통해 개선될 수 있는 유명인과 공인의 모습을 복제하는 AI의 오용 문제가 점점 더 커지고 있다고 생각합니다. 특히 초현실적인 이미지와 딥페이크 생성에 있어 AI의 발전으로 유명인들은 그들의 이미지가 동의 없이 사용되어 그들의 평판이 훼손될 위험에 처해 있습니다. 부도덕한 사용자들이 자신의 신원을 왜곡하는 AI 생성 콘텐츠를 만들어 개인정보 침해와 명예훼손으로 이어질 수 있습니다. 따라서, 이러한 유해한 관행으로부터 개인을 보호하기 위한 규정이 마련되어야 하며, AI가 사람들의 공공 이미지를 착취하거나 조작하는 데 사용되지 않도록 해야 합니다. 이는 윤리적 기준을 준수하는 동시에 혁신과 책임의 균형을 맞출 것입니다.

어휘

likeness n 닮음, 초상 | **public figure** 공인 | **strict** adj 엄격한 | **hyper-realistic** adj 초현실적인 | **deepfake** n 딥페이크 | **consent** n 동의 | **reputation** n 명성 | **unscrupulous** adj 부도덕한 | **identity** n 정체성 | **defamation** n 명예 훼손 | **exploit** v 이용하다 | **manipulate** v 조작하다 | **uphold** v 지키다, 유지하다 | **accountability** n 책임

Actual Test 05

본서 | p. 70

Question 1

Reading Passage

In order to attract qualified teachers, schools in many poor and rural areas offer signing bonuses. These financial incentives are a vital investment in the future of students, and as such should be continued.

자격이 있는 교사들을 유치하기 위해 많은 가난한 시골 지역에서는 사이닝 보너스를 제공한다. 이 금전적 인센티브는 학생들의 미래에 대한 필수적인 투자이며, 따라서 지속되어야 한다.

The main issue that schools in low-income areas face is attracting teachers to work at them. Public schools are funded by state income tax revenue, which means that their budgets are determined by the average income in their area. Therefore, the pay for teachers in poor areas is typically low, which makes it difficult to attract new teachers. So, by providing higher incomes, signing bonuses allow these schools to attract teachers that would otherwise teach in higher income areas.

저소득 지역에 있는 학교들이 당면한 주요한 문제는 그곳에 와서 근무할 교사들을 유치하는 것이다. 공립 학교들은 주 정부의 소득세 세입 지원을 받는데, 이는 그들의 예산이 그 지역의 평균 임금에 의해 정해진다는 의미다. 따라서 가난한 지역의 교사 급여는 보통 낮고, 이것은 새로운 교사들을 유치하는 것을 어렵게 만든다. 그래서 사이닝 보너스는 더 높은 급여를 제공함으로써 이러한 학교들이 고소득 지역에서 가르치려 하는 교사들을 데려올 수 있도록 한다.

The increased salaries that signing bonuses create also attract people from other industries. Many people who are interested in teaching choose not to due to the low average salary that teaching offers. Instead, they pursue other careers in their area of study. For example, scientists working for private corporations can make far more money than they would by teaching science to students. Higher wages can attract these experts to lower income schools in their area where they would not normally consider working.

사이닝 보너스로 늘어난 급여는 또한 다른 산업의 사람들도 유치한다. 가르치는 것에 관심이 있는 많은 사람은 일반적으로 교사의 급여가 낮기 때문에 가르치려고 하지 않는다. 대신 그들은 자신의 학문 분야에서 다른 커리어를 추구한다. 예를 들어, 사기업에서 일하는 과학자들은 학생들에게 과학을 가르치는 것보다 훨씬 더 많은 돈을 벌 수 있다. 더 높은 임금은 이러한 전문가들을 평소라면 일하는 것을 고려해 보지 않았을 저소득 지역의 학교로 유치할 수 있을 것이다.

Signing bonuses are also beneficial because they encourage teachers to remain at one institution for a longer period of time. Most of the institutions stipulate that the teacher must teach for a specific number of years in order to receive their bonus. Many also divide the bonus up between the stipulated years in order to motivate the teacher

사이닝 보너스는 또한 교사들이 한 학교에서 오랫동안 머무르게 하므로 유익하다. 대부분의 학교에서는 교사가 보너스를 받기 위해 일정 기간 동안 가르쳐야 한다고 규정하고 있다. 또한 많은 학교에서 교사들을 더 오래 머물게 하려고 명기된 연수별로 보너스를 나누어서 준다. 이는 학교가 교사들을 더 오래 보유할 수 있도록 하고 학생들에게 안정적인 환경을 제공한다.

to stay longer. This allows the schools to retain their teachers longer, and provides a stable environment for their students.

어휘

qualified adj 자격이 있는 | **signing bonus** (계약 체결 시 선지급하는) 사이닝 보너스 | **income tax** 소득세 | **revenue** n 세입 | **wage** n 임금 | **stipulate** v 규정하다, 명기하다 | **divide up** 분배하다, 분담하다 | **retain** v 보유하다

Lecture Script

AT05

In the reading, the author details the benefits of providing signing bonuses to teachers. As well intentioned as this practice is, it fails to fully address the problems faced by both the schools and the teachers.

지문에서 저자는 교사들에게 사이닝 보너스를 제공하는 것의 이점에 대해 열거하고 있습니다. 이것을 실시하는 것의 의도는 좋으나 학교 측과 교사 측이 당면한 문제들을 완전히 해결하지는 못합니다.

First, he focuses on the fact that schools in low-income areas offer proportionately low salaries. While this is true, it fails to address the reasons that most teachers give for leaving or avoiding such teaching positions altogether. Usually, they cite the quality of facilities and the lack of an effective support system as their motivation for leaving a teaching position. Providing a signing bonus does not address these issues, but spending that money on teaching aids and mentoring programs would.

첫째, 저자는 저소득 지역에 있는 학교들이 비교적 낮은 임금을 지급한다는 사실에 주목합니다. 이는 사실이지만 대부분의 교사가 그러한 교사직을 떠나거나 피하는 이유를 설명하지 못하고 있습니다. 보통 그들은 교사직을 떠나게 되는 동기로 시설의 질과 효과적인 지원 시스템의 부재를 들고 있습니다. 사이닝 보너스를 제공하는 것은 이러한 문제점을 해결하지 않지만, 그 돈을 교구와 멘토링 프로그램에 사용한다면 문제를 해결할 수 있을 것입니다.

Second, he says that signing bonuses can attract people from other industries to the profession of teaching. He claims that the main factor discouraging experts from teaching is the low salary, but when surveyed, most people say that the biggest obstacle to becoming a teacher is the certification process. Specifically, people are discouraged by the amount of time it takes to become certified. In most states, it takes a full year of classes and student teaching to become a certified teacher, which is an investment that a signing bonus does little to offset.

둘째, 저자는 사이닝 보너스가 다른 산업군에서 교사직으로 사람들을 끌어올 수 있다고 말합니다. 그는 전문가들이 교사직을 꺼리는 주요 요인이 낮은 임금이라고 주장하지만, 설문조사를 해보니 대부분의 사람들은 교사가 되는 데 가장 큰 장애물이 자격 취득 과정이라고 답했습니다. 특히 사람들은 자격증을 취득하기까지 걸리는 시간 때문에 의욕을 잃는다고 합니다. 대부분의 주에서 자격증을 가진 교사가 되려면 수업과 실습에 만 1년이 걸리는데, 이것은 사이닝 보너스가 상쇄할 수 없는 투자입니다.

Third, he states that signing bonuses encourage teachers to stay at one school longer. However, studies have shown that the majority of teachers who receive signing bonuses do not fulfill their contractual obligations. Moreover, should we really try to force teachers to stay somewhere they do not want to be? Employees who do not like their workplace are unlikely to put much effort into their work, so keeping them around would be counterproductive.

셋째, 저자는 사이닝 보너스가 교사들이 한 학교에 더 오래 머무르게 장려한다고 언급합니다. 하지만 연구에 따르면 사이닝 보너스를 받는 교사들의 대다수가 계약 의무 기간을 채우지 못합니다. 게다가 교사들이 머물고 싶어 하지 않는 곳에 머물도록 우리가 정말 강요해야만 하는 걸까요? 자신의 일터를 좋아하지 않는 근로자들은 업무에 큰 노력을 기울이지 않으므로 그들을 잡아두는 것은 역효과를 낼 것입니다.

어휘

detail v 상세히 열거하다 | **practice** n 실행, 관행 | **proportionately** adv 비교적으로, 비례해서 | **cite** v (이유를) 들다 | **teaching aid** 교구, 교재 | **obstacle** n 장애물 | **certification** n 자격증, 증명 | **full year** 만 1년 | **offset** v 상쇄하다 | **counterproductive** adj 역효과를 낳는

Sample Summary

Both the reading and lecture talk about providing signing bonuses to attract teachers in poor or rural areas. The reading provides three reasons why it is beneficial, while the lecturer says that giving signing bonuses to teachers does not solve those problems in an effective way.

지문과 강의는 둘 다 저소득 지역이나 시골 지역에 교사들을 유치하기 위해 사이닝 보너스를 제공하는 것에 관해 이야기하고 있다. 지문은 그것이 왜 유익한지에 대해 세 가지 이유를 제시하고 있지만, 강의자는 교사들에게 사이닝 보너스를 주는 것이 문제를 효과적으로 해결하지 못한다고 말한다.

Firstly, the reading states that providing signing bonuses can attract more teachers to schools in low-income areas by providing higher salaries. However, the lecturer undermines this idea by pointing out that the main reasons teachers avoid those schools are the low quality of facilities and the lack of an effective support system. It would be better to spend the money on improving teaching aids and programs.

첫째, 지문은 사이닝 보너스 제공이 더 높은 급여를 제공하여 저소득 지역의 학교로 더 많은 교사를 끌어들일 수 있다고 주장한다. 그러나 강의자는 교사들이 이런 학교를 피하는 주된 이유가 시설의 낮은 질과 효율적인 지원 시스템의 부재라는 점을 지적하며 이 주장을 약화시킨다. 그 돈을 교구와 프로그램을 개선하는 데 사용하면 더 나을 것이다.

Secondly, the reading passage argues that signing bonuses can bring experts from different industries into teaching. However, the lecturer argues back by providing survey data. The survey showed that most experts avoided teaching not because of the low salary, but because of the process of becoming certified as a teacher.

둘째, 지문은 사이닝 보너스가 다른 분야에서 전문가들을 교사직으로 불러올 수 있다고 주장한다. 그러나 강의자는 설문 자료를 제시하며 그 논리를 반박한다. 설문조사는 대부분의 전문가가 낮은 급여 때문이 아니라 교사 자격증을 얻는 과정 때문에 교사직을 피한다는 것을 보여주었다.

Lastly, the reading says that signing bonuses can encourage teachers to remain at one institution for a longer time. This is because teachers must teach for a specific period of time to receive their bonus. However, the lecturer says that the majority of teachers who are provided with signing bonuses actually do not fulfill their contractual obligations. Also, this forced residency will eventually make them less motivated and less productive.

마지막으로, 지문은 사이닝 보너스가 교사들로 하여금 한 학교에 더 오래 머무르도록 장려한다고 이야기한다. 보너스를 받기 위해서는 교사들이 일정 기간 동안 가르쳐야 하기 때문이다. 그러나 강의자는 사이닝 보너스를 받은 대다수 교사가 실제로 계약 의무 기간을 채우지 못한다고 말한다. 이런 강제적인 전속 계약은 결국 교사들의 의욕과 생산성을 떨어뜨리게 될 것이다.

어휘

undermine v 약화시키다 | **certified** adj 증명된, 면허증을 가진 | **contractual** adj 계약의 | **forced** adj 강제적인, 강요된 | **residency** n 거주, 전속

Question 2

Academic Discussion Task

Your professor is teaching a class. Write a post responding to the professor's question.

당신의 교수님께서 강의 중입니다. 교수님의 질문에 답하는 글을 쓰세요.

In your response, you should:
- express and support your opinion
- make a contribution to the discussion

- 당신의 의견을 표현하고 뒷받침하세요
- 토론에 기여하세요

An effective response will contain at least 100 words.
You will have 10 minutes to write it.

효과적인 답변은 최소한 100단어를 포함할 것입니다.
당신은 10분 동안 글을 작성할 수 있습니다.

Dr. Emily: In our recent classes, we've been discussing the use of weight-loss drugs. There is a significant debate about their role. Some people see these drugs as a quick fix to a complicated problem, while others argue they can provide the necessary support for people struggling with weight-related health issues. Would you support weight-loss drugs or lifestyle changes?

에밀리 교수: 최근 수업에서 우리는 체중 감량 약물의 사용에 대해 논의했습니다. 약물의 역할에 대해 상당한 논쟁이 있습니다. 어떤 사람들은 이러한 약물을 복잡한 문제에 대한 빠른 해결책으로 보는 반면, 다른 사람들은 체중 관련 건강 문제로 어려움을 겪고 있는 사람들에게 필요한 지원을 제공할 수 있다고 주장합니다. 체중 감량 약물을 지지하시나요, 아니면 생활 습관 변화를 지지하시나요?

Jaslene: I believe promoting lifestyle changes is more effective than relying on weight-loss drugs. While these drugs might offer short-term results, they often come with side effects and

자슬린: 저는 체중 감량 약물에 의존하기보다는 생활 습관 변화를 촉진하는 것이 더 효과적이라고 생각합니다. 이러한 약물들은 단기적인 결과를 제공할 수 있지만, 종종 부작용이 따르고 장기적인 체중

don't support long-term weight management. Sustainable weight loss comes from healthier eating habits and regular exercise, which not only help maintain a healthy weight but also improve overall well-being. Focusing on lifestyle changes can lead to lasting benefits, such as better heart health and increased energy, making it a more reliable approach than depending on medication alone.

관리에는 도움이 되지 않습니다. 지속 가능한 체중 감량은 더 건강한 식습관과 규칙적인 운동에서 비롯되며, 이는 건강한 체중을 유지할 뿐만 아니라 전반적인 웰빙을 개선하는 데도 기여합니다. 생활 습관 변화에 집중하면 심장 건강 개선이나 에너지 증가와 같은 장기적인 이득을 얻을 수 있어 약물에만 의존하는 것보다 더 신뢰할 수 있는 접근 방식이 됩니다.

Alexander: While I agree with Jaslene's point that lifestyle changes are important, I think weight-loss drugs can play a helpful role for certain individuals. For example, some people face genetic or medical challenges that make losing weight difficult, even with diet and exercise. In these cases, weight-loss drugs can offer valuable support. Rather than dismissing their use, I believe they can be part of a comprehensive approach to weight management, particularly for those who struggle with conventional methods. In the end, isn't it better to help people actually lose weight and maintain it through drugs rather than watch them fail using methods that don't work for them?

알렉산더: 저는 자슬린의 생활 습관 변화가 중요하다는 의견에 동의하지만, 체중 감량 약물이 특정 개인에게는 도움이 될 수 있다고 생각합니다. 예를 들어, 일부 사람들은 유전적 또는 의학적 문제로 인해 식단과 운동으로도 체중을 줄이기 어려운 경우가 있습니다. 이러한 상황에서는 체중 감량 약물이 중요한 지원을 제공할 수 있습니다. 이 약물의 사용을 무조건 배제하기보다는, 특히 일반적인 방법으로 어려움을 겪는 사람들에게는 포괄적인 체중 관리 접근법의 일부가 될 수 있다고 생각합니다. 결국, 효과가 없는 방법을 시도하다 실패하는 것을 지켜보는 것보다 약물을 통해 사람들이 실제로 체중을 감량하고 유지하도록 돕는 것이 더 낫지 않을까요?

어휘

drug n 약물 | **debate** n 논쟁 | **support** n 지원 | **promote** v 촉진하다 | **effective** adj 효과적인 | **rely** v 의존하다 | **short-term** adj 단기적인 | **result** n 결과 | **side effect** 부작용 | **long-term** adj 장기적인 | **sustainable** adj 지속 가능한 | **maintain** v 유지하다 | **well-being** n 행복, 건강 | **lasting** adj 지속적인 | **benefit** n 이득 | **genetic** adj 유전적인 | **medical** adj 의학의 | **valuable** adj 가치 있는 | **dismiss** v 묵살하다 | **comprehensive** adj 종합적인 | **approach** n 접근법 | **conventional** adj 전통적인 | **method** n 방법 | **fail** v 실패하다

Sample Response

I tend to agree with Jaslene on this issue. While weight-loss drugs might offer quick results, they're often temporary solutions with potential side effects. Even if individuals lose weight, it's likely to return once they stop taking the medication. In contrast, sustainable weight management lies in

저는 이 문제에 대해 자슬린의 의견에 더 동의하는 편입니다. 체중 감량 약물은 빠른 결과를 제공할 수 있지만, 대부분 부작용이 따르는 일시적인 해결책입니다. 설령 체중을 감량하더라도, 약물 복용을 중단하면 다시 체중이 늘어날 가능성이 큽니다. 반면, 지속 가능한 체중 관리는 균형 잡힌 식단과 규칙적

lifestyle changes like a balanced diet and regular exercise, which improve both weight and overall health. For example, exercise can help people alleviate stress and boost cardiovascular health. That said, I understand Alexander's view that certain individuals may need weight-loss drugs due to specific health conditions. In these cases, careful medical supervision is essential to ensure their safe and effective use.

인 운동과 같은 생활 방식의 변화에 있으며, 이는 체중뿐만 아니라 전반적인 건강을 개선합니다. 예를 들어, 운동은 스트레스를 완화하고 심혈관 건강을 증진시킬 수 있습니다. 그렇긴 하지만, 특정 건강 상태로 인한 일부 사람들이 체중 감량 약물이 필요할 수도 있다는 알렉산더의 견해를 이해합니다. 이러한 경우에는 안전하고 효과적인 사용을 보장하기 위해 신중한 의학적 감독이 필수적입니다.

어휘

temporary adj 일시적인 | **solution** n 해결책 | **potential** adj 잠재적인 | **alleviate** v 완화하다 | **boost** v 증진시키다 | **cardiovascular** adj 심혈관의 | **condition** n 상태 | **supervision** n 감독 | **effective** adj 효과적인

Actual Test 06

본서 | p. 74

Question 1

Reading Passage

Historically, the British Isles were invaded by many foreign forces such as the Celts, the Romans, and the Angles and Saxons. In light of this history, it is easy to see why it is unclear whom the people of England are descended from. However, there is strong evidence that points to the Anglo-Saxons as the ancestors of the majority of modern English people.

역사적으로 영국 제도는 켈트족, 로마인, 앵글족 및 색슨족과 같은 여러 외적의 침입을 받았다. 이러한 역사적인 면에서 보면 영국인들이 누구의 후손인지 명확하지 않은 이유를 쉽게 알 수 있다. 그러나 현대 영국인들 대부분의 선조가 앵글로 색슨족이라는 것을 가리키는 강력한 증거가 있다.

To begin with, historical records show that the movement of the Anglo-Saxons to the British Isles was a resettlement. They left their former homes on the mainland in what is now Germany and Denmark and came to England, which was inhabited by Celtic tribes. Written accounts from around that time give the impression that this wave of immigration quickly overwhelmed the Celts and forced them to retreat into what is now Wales and Scotland.

우선, 역사적인 기록을 보면 앵글로 색슨족이 영국 제도로 이주한 것이 재정착이었다는 것을 알 수 있다. 그들은 지금의 독일과 덴마크에 해당하는 본토인 그들의 고향을 떠나 켈트족이 살고 있던 영국으로 왔다. 그 시대의 문자 기록은 이러한 이민의 물결이 켈트족을 압도했으며 그들을 지금의 웨일스와 스코틀랜드로 후퇴하게 했다는 인상을 준다.

This is further supported by the fact that English developed from the language of the Anglo-Saxons and not the earlier Celts. A simple comparison of English with Welsh or Gaelic, both Celtic tongues, clearly shows how drastically different these languages are. As the Anglo-Saxons exerted their dominance over the island, their language replaced those of the Celtic peoples. This linguistic shift increases the likelihood that today's population came from the Germanic invaders.

이는 더 나아가 영어가 초기의 켈트어가 아닌 앵글로 색슨족의 언어로부터 발달했다는 사실에 의해 뒷받침된다. 영어를 켈트어에 해당하는 웨일스어나 게일어와 단순히 비교해 보면 이 언어들이 얼마나 크게 다른지 명백히 알 수 있다. 앵글로 색슨족이 섬에서 권력을 행사함에 따라 그들의 언어는 켈트인의 언어를 대신했다. 이러한 언어적 변화는 오늘날의 인구가 게르만족 침략자들의 후손일 가능성을 높인다.

Even more conclusive proof was gained by studying the DNA of people living in several villages in eastern England. Their DNA was compared to samples from modern people with Celtic and Germanic backgrounds, and it was

훨씬 더 결정적인 증거는 영국 동부의 여러 마을에 사는 사람들의 DNA를 조사한 결과에서 나왔다. 그들의 DNA를 켈트족과 게르만족 배경을 가진 현대인들의 표본과 비교했는데, 이것이 앵글로 색슨족의 이동이 시작된 지역에 사는 사람들의 것과 거의

found to be almost identical to that of people living in the areas where the Anglo-Saxon migration began. This provides inarguable proof that the people of modern-day England are more closely related to the Anglo-Saxons than to the original Celtic population.

같다는 것이 밝혀졌다. 이것은 현대 영국인들이 원래의 켈트족보다는 앵글로 색슨족과 더 밀접히 관련되어 있다는 명백한 증거를 제공한다.

어휘

be descended from ~의 자손이다 | **ancestor** n 조상 | **resettlement** n 재정착 | **retreat** v 후퇴하다 | **Welsh** n 웨일스어 | **Gaelic** n 게일어 | **drastically** adv 크게, 대폭 | **exert** v 가하다, 행사하다 | **likelihood** n 가능성 | **Germanic** adj 게르만(인)의, 게르만어족의 | **conclusive** adj 결정적인 | **inarguable** adj 명백한

Lecture Script

AT06

I trust you read the article I sent? Although much of the historical information included in that article is factual, the conclusions that the author drew from his examples are far from accurate. It is more likely that the most of the population of modern-day England are descended from the Celts whom the Anglo-Saxons subjugated.

제가 여러분에게 보낸 글을 읽었겠죠? 그 글에 포함된 역사 정보의 대부분은 사실이지만 저자가 예시에서 도출한 결론은 정확함과는 거리가 멉니다. 현대 영국 인구의 대부분은 앵글로 색슨족이 지배했던 켈트족의 후손일 가능성이 훨씬 더 큽니다.

The author is correct in asserting that the Celtic people were invaded by the Anglo-Saxons. However, the sources that the author mentions were written by the invaders, who had no way to accurately gauge the number of Celts living in the British Isles at that time. Instead, modern historians believe that the Anglo-Saxon population was dwarfed by the native Celts after the Battle of Badon Hill. So, it is unlikely that the Celtic population could have been so completely forced out.

켈트족이 앵글로 색슨족의 침입을 받았다는 저자의 주장은 맞습니다. 하지만 저자가 언급한 자료는 침략자들에 의해 쓰였는데, 그들은 당시 영국 제도에 살던 켈트족의 수를 정확히 측정할 방법이 없었습니다. 오히려 현대 역사가들은 Badon Hill의 전투 이후 앵글로 색슨족 인구가 켈트 원주민에 의해 위축되었다고 생각하죠. 따라서 켈트족 인구가 그렇게 완전히 쫓겨났다는 것은 있을 수 없어요.

He also cites the fact that the Anglo-Saxon language became the language of the realm as further evidence of population replacement. When one culture becomes ruled by another, its people will often adopt the oppressors' language. This is clearly demonstrated by the expansion of the Roman Empire. As various cultures around the

저자는 또한 인구 대체의 추가적 증거로 앵글로 색슨어가 그 지역의 언어가 되었다는 사실을 인용하고 있습니다. 하나의 문화가 다른 문화에 지배를 받으면 사람들은 종종 정복자의 언어를 받아들이게 됩니다. 이는 로마 제국의 확장에 의해 분명히 입증되고 있습니다. 지중해 연안의 많은 문화가 제국에 흡수되면서 그들은 라틴어를 새로운 언어로 받아들

Mediterranean were absorbed by the empire, they adopted Latin as their new language. However, that does not mean that their population was replaced with people of Latin ancestry, nor does the adoption of Anglo-Saxon mean that the Celts were replaced.

였습니다. 하지만 그것이 인구가 라틴 선조를 가진 사람들로 대체되었다는 의미는 아닙니다. 역시 앵글로 색슨어의 채택이 켈트족이 앵글로 색슨족으로 대체되었다는 뜻은 아니죠.

In his final example, the author cites a DNA study, but I have doubts about the way in which the study was carried out. The study was conducted in one small region of eastern England. Since that region is close to the European mainland, it is not surprising to find a strong Anglo-Saxon influence there. However, it is unrealistic to assume that such a small, localized sample could give an accurate representation of the genetic history of the whole nation's population. Indeed, other studies conducted in different parts of the country have shown much closer resemblance to modern Celtic people.

마지막 예에서 저자는 DNA 연구를 인용하는데, 저는 그 연구가 행해진 방식에 의혹을 하고 있습니다. 그 연구는 영국 동부의 작은 지역에서 시행됐습니다. 그 지역은 유럽 본토와 가까우므로 그곳에서 강력한 앵글로 색슨의 영향을 발견하는 것은 놀라운 일이 아닙니다. 그러나 그처럼 작고 국지적인 표본이 전체 국가 인구의 유전 역사를 정확히 대표한다고 가정하는 것은 비현실적이에요. 사실 영국의 다른 지역에서 시행된 연구들은 현대 켈트인과 훨씬 더 가까운 유사성을 보입니다.

어휘

factual adj 사실에 기반을 둔 | **subjugate** v 지배하다 | **gauge** v 측정하다, 추정하다 | **dwarf** v 위축하다 | **localized** adj 국지적인 | **genetic** adj 유전(학)의 | **resemblance** n 유사성, 닮음

Sample Summary

Both the reading and lecture talk about the ancestry of modern-day English people. The reading suggests they are descended from Anglo-Saxons. However, the lecturer contradicts this by arguing that modern English people are actually descendants of Celts, not Anglo-Saxons.

지문과 강의는 둘 다 현대 영국인들의 혈통에 관해 이야기하고 있다. 지문에서는 그들이 앵글로 색슨족의 후손이라고 말한다. 그러나 강의자는 현대 영국인들이 실제로 앵글로 색슨족이 아니라 켈트족의 후손이라고 주장하며 이를 반박한다.

Firstly, the reading quotes written records of that time which state that the majority of Anglo-Saxons migrated from Europe to England, quickly overwhelming the native Celts. However, the lecturer undermines the historical accuracy of the records, by pointing out that the accounts

첫째, 지문은 그 당시의 기록을 인용하는데, 그 기록은 앵글로 색슨족의 대부분이 유럽에서 영국으로 이동했으며, 켈트 원주민을 빠르게 압도했다고 언급하고 있다. 그러나 강의자는 그 기록이 침략자들에 의해 쓰였다는 점을 지적하면서 기록의 역사적 정확성을 약화시킨다. 사실 켈트족은 침략자들보다

were written by the invaders. In fact, the Celts outnumbered their invaders.

수적으로 우세했다.

Secondly, the author points out the similarities between modern English and the Anglo-Saxon language. He says that this would only have been possible if Anglo-Saxons were the primary population living in Britain. However, the lecturer argues that this does not lead to the conclusion that the people using the Anglo-Saxon language were in fact Anglo-Saxons. Rather, the Celts merely adopted the language of the invaders, just as Latin was used throughout the Roman Empire.

둘째, 저자는 현대 영어와 앵글로 색슨어 간의 유사점에 주목한다. 그는 이것이 앵글로 색슨족이 영국에 사는 주요 주민이었을 때에만 가능했을 것이라고 말한다. 그러나 강의자는 이것이 앵글로 색슨어를 사용하는 사람들이 실제로 앵글로 색슨족이었다는 결론으로 이어지지는 않는다고 주장한다. 오히려 라틴어가 로마 제국 전역에서 사용된 것처럼 켈트족이 침략자의 언어를 받아들였을 뿐이다.

Lastly, the reading shares a DNA test result, which shows that people currently living in eastern England have DNA almost identical to the Anglo-Saxons. However, the lecturer points out that this localized sample cannot be an accurate representation of the entire population. The lecturer also says that there are results from other studies in which people living in modern-day England have DNA that closely resembles modern Celts.

마지막으로, 지문은 DNA 검사 결과를 공유하는데, 이는 현재 영국 동부에 사는 사람들이 앵글로 색슨족과 거의 같은 DNA를 가지고 있다는 것을 보여준다. 그러나 강의자는 이런 국지적인 표본이 전체 인구를 정확히 대표할 수 없다는 점을 지적한다. 강의자는 또한 현대 영국에 사는 사람들이 현대 켈트족과 매우 닮은 DNA를 가지고 있다는 것을 보여주는 연구 결과가 있다고 말한다.

어휘

ancestry n 가계, 혈통 | **invader** n 침략자 | **outnumber** v 수적으로 우세하다

Question 2

Academic Discussion Task

Your professor is teaching a class. Write a post responding to the professor's question.

당신의 교수님께서 강의 중입니다. 교수님의 질문에 답하는 글을 쓰세요.

In your response, you should:

- express and support your opinion
- make a contribution to the discussion

- 당신의 의견을 표현하고 뒷받침하세요
- 토론에 기여하세요

An effective response will contain at least 100 words.
You will have 10 minutes to write it.

효과적인 답변은 최소한 100단어를 포함할 것입니다.
당신은 10분 동안 글을 작성할 수 있습니다.

Dr. Noah: Some people think that governments should provide financial support to encourage higher birth rates, while others believe that social policies, such as better childcare and parental leave, are more effective. What are your thoughts on this?

노아 교수: 어떤 사람들은 정부가 출산율을 높이기 위해 재정적 지원을 제공해야 한다고 생각하는 반면, 어떤 사람들은 더 나은 보육 및 육아 휴직과 같은 사회 정책이 더 효과적이라고 생각합니다. 이에 대해 어떻게 생각하시나요?

Eva: In my opinion, investing in better childcare facilities would be the most effective strategy to boost birth rates. The high cost and limited availability of quality childcare are significant concerns for many potential parents. By providing affordable, high-quality childcare options, we could make it easier for people to balance work and family life. This support would relieve some of the financial pressure and make parenthood more accessible to a broader range of people, potentially encouraging more families to have children and contributing to increased birth rates.

에바: 제 의견으로는 더 나은 보육 시설에 투자하는 것이 출산율을 높이기 위한 가장 효과적인 전략이라고 생각합니다. 많은 잠재적인 부모들에게는 양질의 보육 서비스가 비싸고 제한적이라는 점이 큰 문제입니다. 저렴하면서도 양질의 보육 옵션을 제공한다면 사람들이 일과 가정생활을 더 쉽게 병행할 수 있을 것입니다. 이러한 지원은 일부 재정적인 부담을 덜어주고 더 많은 사람들이 부모가 되는 것을 가능하게 하며, 궁극적으로 더 많은 가정이 자녀를 가질 수 있도록 장려하고 출산율 증가에 기여할 수 있을 것입니다.

John: I agree with Eva that having better childcare facilities might be helpful for many parents. However, I believe providing generous maternity and paternity leave would be the best way to boost birth rates. A well-structured parental leave policy would give parents the necessary time to bond with their newborns without worrying about their job security or financial stability. This would make parenthood more attractive to many people, as they wouldn't feel pressured to immediately return to work. Also, giving parents the time and support they need during the early stages of parenthood could make the idea of having children more appealing.

존: 저도 더 나은 보육 시설이 많은 부모들에게 도움이 될 것이라는 에바의 의견에 동의합니다. 하지만, 출산율을 높이기 위한 최선의 방법은 관대한 출산 휴가와 육아 휴직을 제공하는 것이라고 믿습니다. 잘 구조화된 부모 휴가 정책은 부모들이 직업 안정성이나 재정적 안정을 걱정하지 않으며, 신생아와 유대감을 형성할 수 있는 시간을 제공합니다. 이는 많은 사람들에게 부모 역할을 더 매력적으로 만들 것이며, 그들이 즉시 직장에 복귀해야 한다는 압박을 느끼지 않도록 해줄 것입니다. 또한 부모가 되는 초기 육아 기간에 필요한 시간과 지원을 제공하면 자녀를 갖는 것이 더 매력적으로 보일 수 있습니다.

어휘

financial adj 재정적인 | **encourage** v 격려하다 | **birth rate** 출생률 | **policy** n 정책 | **childcare** n 보육 | **parental** adj 부모의 | **effective** adj 효과적인 | **invest** v 투자하다 | **facility** n 시설 | **availability** n 이용 가능성 | **significant** adj 중요한 | **affordable** adj 저렴한 | **childcare** n 보육 | **balance** v 균형을 맞추다 | **financial pressure** 재정적 부담 | **parenthood** n 부모로서의 신분 | **accessible** adj 접근 가능한 | **encourage** v 장려하다 | **contribute to** ~에 기여하다 | **generous** adj 관대한 | **maternity leave** (여성의) 출산 휴가 | **paternity leave** (남성의) 육아 휴직 | **bond** v 유대감을 형성하다 | **newborn** n 신생아 | **job security** 직업 안정성 | **stability** n 안정 | **support** n 지원 | **appealing** adj 매력적인

Actual Test 06

Sample Response

While I understand John's point of view, I, like Eva, believe investing in better childcare facilities would be the most effective way to boost birth rates. While parental leave is important, it is a temporary solution. Once parents return to work, the ongoing challenge of balancing career and family life becomes a major barrier. High-quality, affordable childcare would offer a long-term solution by easing the burden on working parents. It would enable more people, especially women, to stay in the workforce while raising children. This could not only alleviate the financial pressure of parenthood but also create a supportive environment where having more children becomes a more feasible and attractive option for families.

저는 존의 관점을 이해하지만, 에바처럼 더 나은 보육 시설에 투자하는 것이 출산율을 높이는 가장 효과적인 방법이라고 생각합니다. 출산 휴가는 중요하지만, 그것은 일시적인 해결책에 불과합니다. 일단 부모들이 다시 직장으로 돌아가면 일과 가정생활의 균형을 맞추는 지속적인 어려움이 큰 장애물이 됩니다. 양질의 저렴한 보육 시설은 일하는 부모들의 부담을 덜어줌으로써 장기적인 해결책을 제공할 수 있습니다. 이는 특히 여성들이 자녀를 양육하면서도 계속해서 직장에 남을 수 있도록 도와줍니다. 이는 부모 역할의 재정적 부담을 완화할 뿐만 아니라, 더 많은 자녀를 갖는 것이 가정에 더 현실적이고 매력적인 선택이 될 수 있는 지원 환경을 조성할 수 있습니다.

어휘

temporary adj 일시적인 | **challenge** n 도전 | **barrier** n 장애물 | **long-term** adj 장기적인 | **workforce** n 노동력 | **alleviate** v 완화하다 | **supportive** adj 지원적인 | **feasible** adj 실현 가능한

Actual Test 07

본서 | p. 78

Question 1

Reading Passage

The technology of genetic modification offers many potential advances, especially in agriculture. The creation of genetically modified organisms (GMOs) is a revolution in science that may allow us to grow sufficient food and even improve a country's economy in the following ways.

유전자 변형 기술은 특히 농업 분야에서 많은 잠재적 발전을 제공한다. 유전자 변형 유기체(GMOs)의 개발은 다음과 같은 방법으로 우리가 충분한 식량을 생산하고 국가 경제까지 개선할 수 있게 하는 과학의 혁명이다.

First, GMOs can resolve one of the most significant difficulties many farmers face: a lack of precipitation. By genetically modifying crops to grow in dry conditions, science could give these farmers a higher yield from their land. If they can grow enough to have a surplus, they can sell the extra at the market. In this way, not only the farmers, but also the local and even the national economy could benefit.

첫째, 유전자 변형 유기체는 많은 농부가 직면한 가장 심각한 어려움 중 하나인 강수량 부족을 해결해 줄 수 있다. 건조한 기후에서 작물이 자라도록 유전적으로 변형함으로써 과학은 농부들이 땅에서 더 높은 생산량을 얻도록 해 준다. 그들이 여분의 농산물을 얻을 만큼 작물을 기르면 그것을 시장에서 팔 수 있다. 이러한 방식으로 농부들뿐 아니라 지역 경제와 심지어 국가 경제에도 도움이 될 수 있다.

Second, another threat that farmers face is pest organisms, particularly insects and fungi. However, GMOs can be created that produce toxins that will protect them against pests and remain harmless to people. With such crops, synthetic pesticides would be unnecessary, which benefits not only consumers, but also the environment. Chemical pesticides are a serious environmental pollutant, and they can affect many species other than the ones they are intended to kill.

둘째, 농부들이 직면한 또 다른 위협은 해충들, 특히 곤충과 곰팡이다. 그러나 스스로를 병충해로부터 보호하고 인간에게는 무해한 독소를 만들어 내는 유전자 변형 유기체를 개발할 수 있다. 그러한 작물들로 인해 합성 살충제는 불필요해질 것이며, 이는 소비자뿐만 아니라 환경에도 이득이 된다. 화학 살충제는 심각한 환경 오염원이며, 박멸하려던 해충이 아닌 다른 종에게도 악영향을 미칠 수 있다.

Third, GMO crops can provide a variety of nutrients for many people who suffer from malnutrition due to their limited diet. These people suffer from vitamin deficiencies that can severely affect their health. However, these GMO crops are able to combat this situation because they can provide nutrients that the plants normally would not

셋째, 유전자 변형 작물은 제한된 식단으로 인해 영양실조로 고생하는 많은 이들에게 다양한 영양소를 제공할 수 있다. 이들은 건강에 심각한 영향을 미칠 수 있는 비타민 부족으로 고생한다. 그러나 유전자 변형 작물은 식물이 일반적으로 포함하고 있지 않은 영양소를 제공할 수 있으므로 이런 상황을 타개할 수 있다. 예를 들어, 많은 문화권에서 쌀을 주

contain. For example, many cultures use rice as their staple crop, but it lacks vitamin A, which is required to grow properly. So, scientists have created a type of rice that contains large amounts of vitamin A to supplement their diet.

요 작물로 이용하고 있지만 쌀에는 제대로 성장하기 위해 필요한 비타민 A가 부족하다. 따라서 과학자들은 그들의 식단을 보충하기 위해 다량의 비타민 A를 함유한 쌀 품종을 개발했다.

어휘

genetic modification 유전자 변형 | **yield** n 생산량, 수확량 | **surplus** n 잉여분 | **fungi** n 곰팡이류 | **synthetic** adj 합성한, 인조의 | **pesticide** n 살충제 | **pollutant** n 오염 물질, 오염원 | **malnutrition** n 영양실조 | **deficiency** n 부족, 결핍 | **staple crop** 주요 작물 | **supplement** v 보충하다

Lecture Script

According to the reading, genetically modified organisms could help people in many ways, particularly with regard to agriculture. However, they may affect other plants and people in ways that the scientists never expected, so we should be very careful about using them.

지문에 따르면 유전자 변형 유기체는 여러 방면에서, 특히 농업과 관련해 사람들에게 도움이 된다고 합니다. 그렇지만 그것은 과학자들이 전혀 예상치 못한 방식으로 다른 식물들과 사람들에게 영향을 미칠 수 있으므로 우리는 그것을 활용하는 것에 매우 주의를 기울여야 합니다.

To begin with, creating crops that can grow in areas that lack water seems like a fantastic idea. Such plants could allow people to grow food in areas that they never could before. But, that means that they could also thrive in areas where we did not intend them to. If they can grow in minimal soil and dry conditions, they could replace the normal plants, altering the food chain. In addition, they could crossbreed with non-GMO plants, making it difficult for people to know if their food is organic or GMO.

우선, 물이 부족한 지역에서 자랄 수 있는 작물을 만들어 내는 것은 환상적인 아이디어처럼 보입니다. 그런 식물들 덕분에 사람들은 절대 불가능했던 곳에서 식량을 재배할 수 있게 되었습니다. 하지만 이는 우리가 의도치 않은 지역에서도 작물이 번성할 수 있다는 의미입니다. 작물이 최소의 토양과 건조한 기후에서 자랄 수 있다면, 정상적인 식물을 대체해 먹이 사슬을 변형시킬 수도 있습니다. 게다가 그런 작물들이 유전자 변형이 되지 않은 식물과 교배되면서 사람들은 자신이 먹는 식품이 유기농인지 유전자 변형 식품인지 알기 어렵게 됩니다.

Next, developing insect and fungi resistant plants also has obvious benefits. Scientists have already created some such as corn and soya bean plants, but they have produced unexpected results. Firstly, it is only a temporary fix because insects reproduce so rapidly that they are already adapting to the toxin. Secondly, the pollen from GMO corn often gets blown onto other plants, where beneficial insects eat it and are poisoned.

다음으로, 곤충과 곰팡이에 저항력이 있는 식물들을 개발하는 것 역시 명백한 이점들이 있습니다. 과학자들은 옥수수와 콩 같은 그런 식물들을 이미 개발했지만 이것은 예상치 못한 결과를 낳았습니다. 첫째, 곤충이 너무 빨리 번식해서 이미 독소에 적응하고 있기 때문에 이는 그저 임시적인 해결책입니다. 둘째, 유전자 변형 옥수수에서 나오는 꽃가루는 종종 다른 식물로 옮겨가는데, 유익한 곤충들이 그것을 먹고 독살됩니다. 이는 특정 종의 나비 개체

This has rapidly reduced the populations of some types of butterflies.

수를 급격히 감소시켰습니다.

Finally, providing adequate nutrition for the millions of people who subsist on poor diets seems difficult to argue against. But, simply adding vitamins to food that would not normally contain them is not a complete solution to the problem. Many experts agree that the plants that normally contain vitamin A such as leafy and root vegetables provide far more benefits than just that nutrient. Plus, the method by which the vitamin has been added could make it useless to people who are allergic to the chemicals that carry the vitamin.

마지막으로, 빈약한 식단으로 연명하는 수백만 명의 사람들에게 적절한 영양을 공급하는 것에 대해서는 반론하기 힘들어 보입니다. 그러나 일반적으로 비타민을 함유하지 않은 식품에 단순히 그 비타민을 첨가하는 것이 그 문제에 대한 완벽한 해결책은 아닙니다. 많은 전문가는 잎줄기채소나 뿌리채소같이 일반적으로 비타민 A를 함유한 식물들이 그 영양소만이 아니라 훨씬 더 많은 이점을 제공한다는 것에 동의합니다. 게다가 비타민을 첨가하는 방식 때문에 비타민을 전달하는 화학물질에 알레르기가 있는 사람들에게는 효과가 없을 수도 있습니다.

어휘

with regard to ~와 관련하여 | **food chain** 먹이 사슬 | **crossbreed** ⓥ 이종 교배하다 | **soya bean** 콩 | **fix** ⓝ 해결책 | **pollen** ⓝ 꽃가루 | **subsist on** ~로 연명하다 | **argue against** 반론하다 | **leafy vegetable** 잎줄기채소 | **root vegetable** 뿌리채소

Sample Summary

The reading gives reasons why genetically modified organisms (GMOs) could be beneficial to humans. However, the lecturer says that we still need to be careful about introducing genetically engineered organisms into the environment because they could bring unexpected results.

지문은 왜 유전자 변형 유기체(GMOs)가 인간에게 유익한지에 대한 이유를 들고 있다. 그러나 강의자는 유전자 조작 유기체가 예측하지 못한 결과를 가져올 수 있으므로 이를 환경에 도입하는 것에 주의할 필요가 있다고 말한다.

Firstly, the author explains that organisms can be modified to survive in regions that have little to no precipitation. This would help the farmers in dry regions. However, the lecturer undermines this idea by pointing out that it could be difficult to keep the plants under control. If the GMOs could thrive that well, they could affect the food chain.

첫째, 저자는 유기체가 강수량이 거의 없거나 아예 없는 지역에서 생존할 수 있도록 변형될 수 있다고 설명한다. 이는 건조한 지역의 농부들에게 도움이 될 것이다. 그러나 강의자는 그 식물을 통제하는 것이 어려울 것이라는 점을 지적하며 이 생각을 약화한다. 유전자 변형 유기체가 그렇게 잘 자랄 수 있다면 먹이 사슬에도 영향을 미칠 것이다.

Secondly, the reading passage cites the fact that GMOs could be developed to produce natural toxins to make them resistant to insects and fungi. This would also decrease the use of pesticides,

둘째, 읽기 지문은 곤충이나 곰팡이에 저항력을 가지는 자연적 독소를 만들어 낼 수 있는 유전자 변형 유기체를 개발할 수 있다는 사실을 인용한다. 이는 살충제의 사용도 줄일 것인데, 이는 더 건강한 작물

which means we could grow healthier crops. However, the lecturer says that insects reproduce so rapidly that they would adapt to the toxin. Also, the pollen from these GMOs could kill beneficial insects.

을 재배할 수 있다는 것을 의미한다. 하지만 강의자는 곤충들이 매우 빨리 번식하기 때문에 이런 독소에 적응할 것이라고 말한다. 또한, 이들 유전자 변형 유기체에서 나오는 꽃가루는 이로운 곤충들을 죽일 수도 있다.

Lastly, the reading argues that GMOs could help people who have limited diets. GMOs could provide them with nutrients that their staple crops lack. However, the lecturer states that this is not a better option because people can consume a greater variety of nutrients by eating other natural foods. Also, the chemicals contained in GMOs could cause allergic reactions in some people.

마지막으로, 지문은 유전자 변형 유기체가 제한된 식단을 가진 사람들을 도울 수 있다고 주장한다. 유전자 변형 유기체는 그들의 주요 작물에 부족한 영양소를 제공할 수 있다. 그러나 강의자는 사람들이 다른 자연식품을 섭취함으로써 더욱 다양한 영양소를 섭취할 수 있기 때문에 이것은 더 나은 선택지가 아니라고 말한다. 또한, 유전자 변형 유기체에 함유된 화학물질들은 일부 사람들에게 알레르기 반응을 일으킬 수도 있다.

어휘

cite v 인용하다, (이유, 예를) 들다 | **allergic reaction** 알레르기 반응

Question 2

Academic Discussion Task

Your professor is teaching a class. Write a post responding to the professor's question.

당신의 교수님께서 강의 중입니다. 교수님의 질문에 답하는 글을 쓰세요.

In your response, you should:
- express and support your opinion
- make a contribution to the discussion

- 당신의 의견을 표현하고 뒷받침하세요
- 토론에 기여하세요

An effective response will contain at least 100 words.
You will have 10 minutes to write it.

효과적인 답변은 최소한 100단어를 포함할 것입니다.
당신은 10분 동안 글을 작성할 수 있습니다.

Dr. Janet: Our class has been examining the ethical implications of consuming and farming animals. Some argue that human consumption necessitates a degree of animal farming, while others advocate for a shift to plant-based diets for ethical and environmental reasons. Some people believe that eating meat is necessary, while others argue that plant-based diets are a better alternative. Do you agree or disagree?

자넷 교수: 우리 수업에서는 육류 소비와 축산의 윤리적 함의를 살펴보고 있습니다. 어떤 사람들은 인간의 소비가 어느 정도의 동물 사육을 필요로 한다고 주장하는 반면, 다른 사람들은 윤리적, 환경적 이유로 식물성 식단으로 전환해야 한다고 주장합니다. 어떤 사람들은 육식이 필요하다고 생각하는 반면, 어떤 사람들은 식물성 식단이 더 나은 대안이라고 주장합니다. 이에 동의합니까, 반대합니까?

Candice: I would encourage a shift toward plant-based diets. Factory farming often involves significant cruelty to animals and is a major contributor to greenhouse gas emissions, which exacerbate environmental issues like climate change. By promoting plant-based diets, we could reduce animal suffering and lower the environmental impact of food production. Additionally, a plant-based diet offers health benefits and introduces more diversity into our meals, helping people explore new, nutritious options. This shift could lead to a more ethical and sustainable approach to feeding the global population.

캔디스: 저는 식물성 식단으로 전환하는 것을 장려합니다. 공장식 축산은 종종 동물에 대한 심각한 학대를 수반하고, 온실가스 배출의 주요 원인으로, 기후 변화와 같은 환경 문제를 악화시킵니다. 식물성 식단을 장려함으로써 동물의 고통을 줄이고, 식량 생산의 환경적 영향을 낮출 수 있습니다. 또한, 식물성 식단은 건강상의 이점을 제공하고, 식단에 더 많은 다양성을 도입해 사람들이 새롭고 영양가 있는 선택사항을 탐색할 수 있도록 돕습니다. 이러한 변화는 글로벌 인구를 먹여 살리는 데 더 윤리적이고 지속 가능한 접근 방식을 가져올 수 있습니다.

Jake: While I understand Candice's viewpoint, I think a balanced approach is far more practical. A complete shift to plant-based diets may not be feasible for everyone due to factors like dietary needs, access to fresh produce, and cultural traditions. Instead of eliminating animal products entirely, I think we should focus on promoting more humane and sustainable farming practices. This approach would address concerns about animal welfare and environmental impact without forcing drastic dietary changes on those who may struggle to adopt a fully plant-based diet. Moderation and mindful consumption are key to making the food system more ethical and sustainable.

제이크: 저는 캔디스의 관점을 이해하지만, 균형 잡힌 접근이 훨씬 더 실용적이라고 생각합니다. 식물성 식단으로의 완전한 전환은 식단 요구, 신선한 농산물에 대한 접근성, 문화적 전통과 같은 요소들로 인해 모두에게 실현 가능하지 않을 수 있습니다. 동물성 제품을 완전히 배제하는 대신, 더 인간적이고 지속 가능한 농업 방식을 장려하는 데 집중해야 한다고 생각합니다. 이러한 접근은 완전한 식물성 식단을 채택하기 어려운 사람들에게 과도한 식단 변화를 강요하지 않으면서, 동물 복지와 환경적 영향에 대한 우려를 해결할 수 있을 것입니다. 절제와 신중한 소비가 더 윤리적이고 지속 가능한 식품 시스템을 만드는 열쇠입니다.

어휘

ethical adj 윤리적인 | **implication** n 영향 | **consumption** n 소비 | **necessitate** v 필요로 하다 | **farming** n 농업 | **advocate** v 옹호하다 | **plant-based** adj 식물성 | **environmental** adj 환경의 | **factory farming** 공장식 축산 | **cruelty** n 잔인함 | **greenhouse gas** n 온실가스 | **emission** n 배출 | **exacerbate** v 악화시키다 | **environmental** adj 환경적인 | **reduce** v 줄이다 | **suffering** n 고통 | **impact** n 영향 | **diversity** n 다양성 | **nutritious** adj 영양가 있는 | **sustainable** adj 지속 가능한 | **balanced** adj 균형 잡힌 | **practical** adj 실용적인 | **feasible** adj 실현 가능한 | **dietary** adj 식이 요법의 | **eliminate** v 제거하다 | **humane** adj 인간적인 | **practice** n 방식 | **welfare** n 복지 | **drastic** adj 과도한 | **moderation** n 절제 | **mindful** adj 신중한 | **consumption** n 소비

Sample Summary

I agree with Jake's balanced approach. While plant-based diets have clear ethical and environmental benefits, expecting everyone to fully give up the animal products that they've been consuming for years isn't realistic or practical for all. However, the current industrial farming system, with its animal cruelty and environmental harm, is not sustainable either. I would advocate for more humane, sustainable farming practices that prioritize animal welfare and reduce environmental damage. At the same time, promoting a reduction in the consumption of animal products could help ease the transition toward a more ethical food system. A combination of these strategies might offer a healthier, more sustainable way forward that is actually achievable for many regular people. This way, we can encourage meaningful progress toward a more ethical food system without imposing unrealistic expectations.

저는 제이크의 균형 잡힌 접근에 동의합니다. 식물성 식단이 윤리적이고 환경적으로 명백한 이점이 있지만, 오랫동안 소비해 온 동물성 제품을 모두 완전히 포기할 것을 모든 사람에게 기대하는 것은 현실적이지도 실용적이지도 않습니다. 그러나 현재의 공장식 축산 시스템은 동물 학대와 환경 파괴를 수반하며, 지속 가능하지도 않습니다. 저는 동물 복지를 우선시하고 환경적 피해를 줄이는 더 인간적이고 지속 가능한 농업 방식을 지지합니다. 동시에, 동물성 제품 소비의 감소를 촉진하는 것은 더 윤리적인 식품 시스템으로의 전환을 수월하게 하는 데 도움이 될 수 있습니다. 이러한 전략들의 조합은일반 사람들에게 실현 가능한, 더 건강하고 지속 가능한 방식으로 나아가는 길을 제시할 수 있습니다. 이러한 방식으로 우리는 비현실적인 기대를 강요하지 않으면서, 더 윤리적인 식품 시스템을 향한 의미 있는 발전을 촉진할 수 있습니다.

어휘

consume v 소비하다, 섭취하다 | **industrial** adj 산업의 | **animal cruelty** 동물 학대 | **harm** n 피해 | **advocate** v 옹호하다 | **prioritize** v 우선시하다 | **reduce** v 줄이다 | **transition** n 전환 | **combination** n 결합 | **strategy** n 전략 | **sustainable** adj 지속 가능한 | **impose** v 강요하다

PAGODA TOEFL

Actual Test

WRITING

PAGODA TOEFL

Actual Test

WRITING

PAGODA TOEFL Actual Test Writing | 해설서